ENTREPRENEURIAL SOUL

39 GROWTH THEMES FOR THE SOUL OF LEADERS AND ENTREPRENEURS

by

Edgar Hernandez Rizek

ENTREPRENEURIAL SOUL

DEDICATION

To my beloved wife, my blood, my veins, my senses, and my strength; who has trusted with a brave heart in this entrepreneur full of passion, with whom she has walked without fear, always united in a single family and under a confident faith.

To my mother, for her dedication body and soul, for her strength, firmness, and dedication.

To my father, for his certainty, conviction, and constant prayer that at some point in my life I would give my whole being to God.

To Pastor Luis Leonor (my uncle), for trusting me and being support of direction and unconditional support from a very early age and for being the man whom God put in my path so that since my adolescence I would know the example of Jesus.

To all the people who put a grain of their talent to make this work come to light.

INTRODUCTION

Entrepreneurial Soul is a devotional and motivational book, composed of various themes focused on the knowledge and spiritual experiences that we live all those who seek to undertake new projects in an increasingly complex and competitive world.

It is a world in which those of us who seek to walk on the path of rightness also live. We are those who feel that we have given everything and that we need an answer to continue. We are in search of truth, morality, and justice because we want to make a better world no matter what we give in return.

The topics I will address below are short, focused, and thoughtful, written in a variety of styles, and are intended to give strength to our souls to undertake each day and to be better leaders of our lives, no matter what circumstances we are living in. They are themes for analysis and represent a call to action, they will serve to bring us closer to the true existence of our God and creator, and the knowledge of his word.

These contents will help us to see other points of view to make better decisions in our professional, family, social, mental, physical, and spiritual development. And they can surely give us an example of what is called to undertake with faith, character, and courage, under-confident obedience and with firm steps, no matter what comes.

Edgar Hernandez Rizek

Autor, Communicator, and Enterpreneur

"You were created to succeed"

edgar@edgarmentor.com

www.edgarmentor.com

edgarhernandezmentor

Edgar Hernández

Rizek edgarhernandezmentor

Table of Contents

The Leadership inside You

"Not so with you. Instead, whoever wants to become great among you must be your servant." **Mark 10:43**

Criticism, loneliness, and rejection are three essential points to define the background and cost of being a leader.

Since leadership cannot be bought, we cannot merely make transactions with it and much less think that we can acquire it by the simple fact of having power, money, or a position. None of these three factors can even peek through the door where the spirit of a true leader dwells.

Those who acquire positions of apparent leadership in any sphere of life and who by their position in the game as bosses, owners, or heads of an organization lead to the festooned socialization, merit and praise, or the closeness of many people, will quickly be replaced or cast aside, and their fruits will not be those of a leader with the right direction.

Since all the great leaders of history have, to a large extent, developed their process in solitude; since those great men we know today in history were rejected in their time; and since at the same time the great voices of change were always attacked by criticism, this

denotes that adversity is an essential part of the growth and future assurance of a magnanimous spirit of leadership.

In the solitude of growing leadership, we find our true selves. It is in this solitude that we break the chains of self and focus on the whole, which is God in its essence. It is here that through meditation we begin little by little, and under solitary pain, to sculpt our character and to know our spiritual side.

In solitude, our old man withers away and we know then the rebirth of a new one, who comes with a renewed mind, who knows, loves his creator and understands the created, one who transforms his frustrated loneliness into love and his immaturity into wisdom and prudence.

Once we break the barrier of loneliness, rejection of our change comes and then the criticisms appear; these will be the best proof that you are sowing again and that this time you will reap great fruits.

It should be emphasized that not everyone who has or assumes a leadership position is a leader, just as there are great leaders who do not have a leading position.

To be called a leader at work, in social life, or family life, requires a set of characteristics and qualities, sometimes innate or acquired that allow the person to reach the position as the result of their actions and the demonstration of being a person with vision, mind, and outstanding capabilities.

The real leader must go ahead, since he is the one who guides and marks the steps previously visualized, thought, and ordered, to the group, or the family. It is the real leader who goes ahead with courage, gallantry, confidence, faith, and winning character, not only to demonstrate and motivate others but also so that his firm and courageous steps are transferred to others with the necessary security to move forward.

For this very reason, the leaders who go ahead are those who, as visible heads, receive the first raindrops that fall and the first dangers that approach, and it is they who lead their own along the path of truth; those leaders of pure character are the ones who go ahead but eat at the end.

Their life is to serve their own with courage and respect, with dedication and passion, giving their life to the service of others; never expecting to be served, nor to take advantage of the strength or power granted to them, because their reward is the satisfaction of serving successfully as a leader, and their joy is to eat and celebrate at the end when all those they lead are satisfied.

School of life

> ***Life is one of the greatest anonymous schools of personal development, in it are hidden the treasures of infinite wisdom, but like any treasure, we must seek it without suffering.***

To walk in life in the right way we must be firm and positive, allowing our will to be governed by the laws that will help us to achieve and give the best of ourselves.

Often, when adverse circumstances happen to us, we become depressed, and momentarily forget all the good things and all the successes that kept us alive in the past, those that life showed us to give us joy while preparing us for the trials that later will bring us pain and sadness.

Even so, it is of utmost importance to recognize that the sadness which comes with hope is what strengthens us and never disappoints us.

Life will always allow us to show what we are, what makes us unique, what no one knows, only you and God.

We were born into this world as light, and the more we learn in the school of life, the more light we can bring to our inner self and others because life is the fuel that keeps the flame of light burning to illuminate our path as well as other people's paths.

It is our commitment to being a light for all those who walk beside us and behind us, and not a stumbling block, no matter what you do, this is everyone's duty. And as you walk and learn in the school of life, remember that it is a school of trial and error.

In this sense, here is a powerful reflection of the 5 elements for victory written by General *Sun Tzu* in his book *The Art of War*:

> ➢ He will win who knows when to fight and when not to fight.

> ➢ He will win who knows how to manage superior and inferior forces.

> ➢ The army animated by the same good spirit in all its ranks will win.

> ➢ If you know the enemy and know yourself, you don't have to fear the outcome of 100 battles.

> ➢ If you know nothing about yourself and the enemy, you will succumb in every battle.

An Entrepreneurial Spirit

If gold does not pass through the fire, its brilliance never comes to it and its roughness weakens its beauty.

We were created with the best materials in the world, our machine is perfect, so much so, that most of the abilities of modern machinery are imitations of different functions of our own body. Let's take the example of the airplane, as we know, the human being was able to invent it by studying the only thing that flew at that time (birds), which like us, are part of the fascinating creation.

We also know as creators that our creator is spectacular.

Humans are truly special, and we must understand the depths of our essence to understand the strength of the foundation on which we build our lives and ideals.

We are the only ones in the world with the ability to think, reason, discern, dream, and interpret; in the end, everything comes from the same place, and that is why we are the only ones with that special spark.

Why were we given that spark? Well, since we were made in the image and likeness of the Creator, He endowed us with the ability to create.

That is why it is well said that "we are the architects of our dreams." By that means we can come to have the dreams that we then shape in our minds and carefully convert to correct their imperfections and, finally, set out on the path of placing within the perfect architecture of the world, and the human network, the work of our hands as a special piece made by a child of the Great Architect.

In the Bible we read in ***Numbers 31: 23-24:***

"…and anything else that can withstand fire must be put through the fire, and then it will be clean. But it must also be purified with the water of cleansing. And whatever cannot withstand fire must be put through that water. On the seventh day wash your clothes and you will be clean. Then you may come into the camp..."

It is an interesting text. The first thing it makes clear to us is: what are the materials can resist, and then it explains it. The gold is us. We are the most precious thing in creation, but to shine in a great banner, we must prepare ourselves to withstand the tests, and then receive the focus of imperishable light that we need to look like gold already melted and worked.

As human beings with an enterprising spirit, we must allow ourselves to be melted by the fire of light. God is the only one who determines how close we must be to the light in order not to fall into error, just as he has determined in his perfect harmony the exact distance of the earth from the sun so that we do not burn to death.

We must be cleansed, withstand the test, the moment, the circumstances, and see ourselves as a piece of gold that will emerge refined and victorious from any fire through which it passes.

We will then be able to endure this experience because the light will allow us to see and know what the end of our endeavor will be. This is how hope will grow and we will begin to feel within ourselves the peace that Daniel (the one in the Bible) felt, as he waited confidently with his companions under the flames of the fire around him, at the moment when the King dictated a death that he never saw.

The final chapter of your entrepreneurship, no matter what you are trying to achieve in life, will be to wash your clothes... and then get clean. It is impossible to reach the ultimate success of your goal with the best decision if you do not have the determination of soul rest.

It is important to believe that we must rest and take the final process with patience, then we must make a reflection, instead of worrying to finish doing... a part that perhaps does not correspond to any of us, because it is God who makes the seed grow.

In the song **Color Esperanza** by *Diego Torres*, a part of the lyrics goes something like this:

"that the windows can be opened, that changing the air will depend on you, changing fears and tempting the future with your heart, that sadness will someday go away, that this is life, it always changes and will change."

Then, when you reach the point of believing that you truly can, from that moment you will have your face painted in the color of hope; when you find the light of the sun of justice that always rises for the just and the unjust, stay in it and do not turn away.

A majestic phrase of **Balthasar G**. that helps us to add one more step to the strength of our entrepreneurial spirit reads:

"Great qualities make great men. A single one of them equals mediocre plurality. There was someone who liked all his things to be great, even the usual objects. In God, everything is immense and infinite. Likewise in a great man, everything must be great and majestic: actions and thoughts will be clothed in a transcendent and grandiose majesty."

Confidence all the way

> *"For I know the plans I have for you," declares the Lord, "plans to prosper you and not to harm you, plans to give you hope and a future."* **Jeremiah 29:11**

To be confident in the future we must believe, to be able to believe we must know, and to know we must live, grow and learn. Now, let me clarify that when I speak of living and learning, I am not referring to the implanted mechanical learning that we live in today, where we are educated as mammalian offspring without reasoning or judgments of our own. I am referring, on the contrary, to the education that comes with life itself, the curiosity for nature, for us human beings, for our creator and his magnificence, and above all, the empirical wisdom that comes with the combination of all these things, a result that is worth more than a thousand academic careers.

It is necessary to know where we come from, where and why we are here in this world, and where we are headed. Only then can we begin to learn what it means in practical terms to walk in hope.

There is no human understanding to decipher our future, but we have the conviction that there is one. Our development as human beings has helped us to see it more clearly; at least it has worked for some of us…

So the problem is not the future, but how we project it, how we walk towards it, how we finalize the path we are on, why we choose it, how we really know if we are doing well; moreover, what tools we need to move forward.

Perhaps we can only see what we all see, but the magic is hidden in thinking about what no one else thinks, for this, we must begin to think. This exercise will allow us to reach creativity, contemplation, and many times innovation.

In essence, every human being is creative and can find a certain liberation through nature. For this reason, we all have the potential to break old chains and find new ways to walk or, in other cases, to completely change the direction of our vision and mission in this life.

Opening our eyes in time is very important because many of us spend our lives without even knowing the reason why we exist.

I have seen elderly people plead to God for the blessing of being able to finish their journey with peace and success. They want the Lord to allow them to see some project of work or life concluded? But I have also seen other elderly people die in nothingness. Although I have seen more young people lost than old people without hope; because those who are currently ending an empty and meaningless life, are the same ones who sowed ignorance in these last generations.

Be willing to take time to pray to God and get to know Him. You must understand how the connection with Him works to obtain gratification, wisdom, peace, and happiness.

We are waiting for the beautiful promise of His coming. This offer has been announced to the billions of us who are waiting for Him today.

Time with God will help our minds to clarify every thought, dusting off unused talents, and making smoother the road ahead.

Baltasar Gracian said:

"Not all who see have opened their eyes, nor do all who look-see. Some begin to see when there is nothing to see; they undo their houses and their things before being a real person. Unhappy the horse whose master lacks eyes, he can hardly grow fat."

If we do not have the will and the desire, it is difficult to receive understanding. And it is even more difficult to want to teach will to those who lack understanding.

One of ***Miguel de Unamuno's*** writings begins with this question, *"What are we going to do on the road as we march?"*

About whatever you are going to do now, my recommendation is that you stop blaming the world for your ineptitudes and negligence and heed the advice of an overcomer of extreme situations, as was ***Elijah (the prophet)***, who when praying to God said:

"Answer me, O Lord, answer me, that this people may know that thou, O LORD, art the God, and that thou turnest their hearts unto thee."

So the important thing is that you walk confidently until you reach the end, enjoy the journey, undertake with the certainty that everything will come in its time, and think that there is someone superior who directs that which is not under your control.

Leadership Qualities

The greatest quality of a leader is service, and it is the shortest path to leadership greatness in any area of life.

Most leaders possess unique qualities and elements, sometimes innate, that differentiate them from others. I want to clarify that in this aspect they are not different because they are more outstanding, intelligent, or more capable in some area; what makes them different is their originality, which makes them unique.

To evaluate the originality of something or someone, we must study their origin. For someone to be able to develop his or her originality, he or she must know what his or her essence is, where it comes from and what it is composed of; that is to say, to know these aspects, study them and learn them.

So, what are the qualities of a leader who knows his origin?

It is worth clarifying that when a leader knows these qualities that we will mention below, he uses his attributes and gifts well, knows his capabilities, and has worked on developing and maturing his talents, which will make him an original person.

Here are the qualities he must have:

> ➢ A leader is original because he knows his origin.

> ➢ A leader is talented because he develops and prepares his capabilities.

> ➢ A leader is unique because he knows his leadership spirit and has mastered his spirit with leadership.

> ➢ A leader is firm because he is courageous, he is not afraid.

> ➢ A leader is capable because he is determined.

> ➢ A leader can only grow because he leads by example and uses his words to motivate.

> ➢ Authentic leaders are not insecure, because their hard self-taught introspection and experiences are the hallmark of their authenticity.

> ➢ A leader possesses the spirit of leadership, he will never lead by position, or with the shield of material goods or the flesh, rather he will speak from within, and direction will come from the heart.

For these reasons, a true leader will not compare himself and much less envy, anyone, because the true leader competes or allies himself strategically, his plans are like works of art and his executions are like tweaks and refinements in the human machinery that moves the world.

The true leader lets his imagination fly, but when it is finished, he goes up and grabs it, makes an agreement with it, puts together a plan that he then creates and executes.

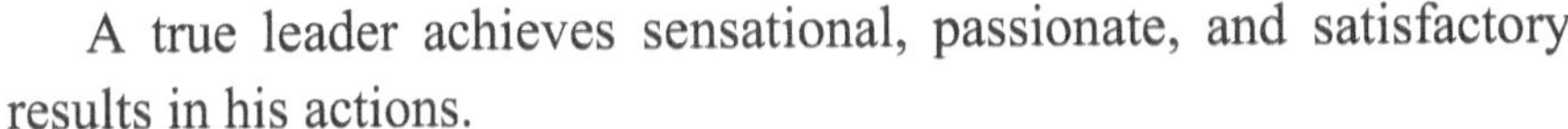

A true leader achieves sensational, passionate, and satisfactory results in his actions.

In a leader, there will always be security, but never ostentatious; there will always be teaching, but never forced; there will always be love, but never feigned; there will always be power and energy, but with prudence. A leader will always be modest, but humble; and willing to lay down his life for those he leads.

Likewise, real leaders make great sacrifices. Thus, every leader who decides to grow with his people must leave behind everything that can be considered an impediment to their good development, regardless of the emotional bond that may exist.

When this leader begins to travel through unknown places for his inner growth and to maximize his capabilities, his load must be light, because when walking through new horizons, he will be able to apply faster tactics to achieve his objectives, since his weight will be much less.

Finally, a great leader, with a mature leadership spirit, will never leave any of his people behind, rather he will lift them up and guide them because they are the foundation and heritage of his vision and mission in this life.

Time and Circumstances

Which came first: circumstances or time?

> *"There is a time for everything, and a season for every activity under the heavens. A time to be born, and a time to die; a time to plant and a time to uproot; a time to weep, and a time to laugh..."'* Ecclesiastes 3.

Time is not ours; we do not control it, it is not within our reach except to see it symbolically, and based on that which we call time, we create our world of planning, goals, life schemes and projections to be carried out in any field.

Time is completely under the command and direction of God, although for Him time does not exist. Even, of the physical things existing in time, it is God who completely determines their existence.

The **Bible** says:

"Therefore I tell you, do not worry about your life, what you will eat or drink; or about your body, what you will wear. Is not life more than food, and the body more than clothes? Look at the birds of the air; they do not sow or reap or store away in barns, and yet your heavenly Father feeds them.

Are you not much more valuable than they?

Can any one of you by worrying add a single hour to your life?"

And as simple as time always moves forward, so time will change things, the forms, the way, the people...

So also, our circumstances will change.

Having understood this, it will be clear in our minds that he who has control of time has dominion over our circumstances. It is he who molds under his supreme intelligence the order of our lives.

Let us be prudent and not be in a hurry to act until the right time comes. We must take one step at a time, even if we know we are ready to run in the Olympics.

We must beware of those things that we allow to catch our attention, and of the impertinences that distract us.

"A time for everything; and everything in its time" I once read.

I once read.

That is why it is necessary to pray to God with heart and reality. For those of us who live in this world of speed and chaos, it does us a lot of good to pray with humility and bow before the Creator.

As we pray to God earnestly for our plans and circumstances, the mind will be enlightened, and the soul healed.

"Do not be like them, for your Father knows what you need before you ask him." **Matthew 6:8**

The action of praying opens and keeps alive a process of communication with the divine, as when in the communication that is stipulated in a marriage the couple always expects an answer; otherwise, a process of breakage could begin.

We must walk confidently, without haste, but being diligent, calm but attentive, leading by the example of Faith, having certainty of what we hope for and conviction of what we do not yet see.

The Final Straight

Getting into the race is easy, but staying in the final stretch with perseverance and optimism is a virtue of few.

Many times we collapse individually or as a couple because all the events we face in this world turned into a materialistic and economically capitalistic bubble; in the same way, many of us are more firm in our dreams.

And the more we nourish ourselves with God, the more convinced we look at the light that guides us together with some people who are joining us along the way.

Let's look at these interesting events in retrospect. Let's look at those of you for whom the family was perhaps the first obstacle in your life. Back then you didn't care what your goal, dream, project, or entrepreneurial desire was. You only sensed that it was a calling, a passion, whereby risking everything for everything, you observed that your choice was not liked by many who could not see what God allowed you to see at that moment.

However, when the maturity of the talents given to each one individually by God himself would reach its point, then in an incredible way but with the feeling of our response, the event you are waiting for would come.

We must be alert, as the word says in the parable of the virgins: *"...ready and with oil in our lamps"*.

We must be different in our walk-through life, we must take risks and be useful to society no matter how long you have been in prison... And when I refer to prison, I am speaking in every sense of the word: prison of the body, prison of the soul, of the mind, or, simply, of the emotions.

We must not degrade our being because we only want to obtain something that can lead us to die in the attempt, and, to our frustration, stay here on Earth. We must give our being in something that, if we die in the attempt, we will carry it stored in our mind and heart, because although we will live eternally, then that attempt will prevail forever.

We were created, we were loved, we sinned and separated, we ate the wrong things and weakened in our development as humans. We killed and abused each other, but in the end, we all know we are connected. We fearlessly persist in defying the divine, then death comes and we have no regrets.

Our life is crude, for that is the way we have drawn it. God, newly in love, painted with perfect brushes the sky, the seas, and us; but when we were seduced we lost our essence and our defects of character and emotion began. How sad the fate of many who serve a good cause, this is a great irony of life.

There is no more courage in this world, there are no more sincere leaders. Perhaps there are some left, so as not to pass judgment on others, but the truth is that most of them are full of fear.

They say, see first to believe first, and my eyes have seen much, but I have seen nothing.

Truly, I am frustrated and dumbfounded for all the human beings who live in the doldrums, for the wretched and abused. And no matter how many you help, more will always come. The task is tireless and I have not even begun, I still feel stupefied and dumbfounded. So many bitter pills, brothers! So many bitter pills!

But with optimism and positivism: Let us all march together to the final stretch, and let us live in this world with love and well-being!

Finding Our Center

If we want to find the central force that gives us balance, mobility and capacity, we must then connect with the divine light, for it is the infinite battery that illuminates and moves our world, it is the only one that provides an imperishable light.

Every day that passes in our lives has a motive that gives sequence to a chain of events that in the end becomes our motivational center, and no matter in which branch of life we apply it we will always have a retroactive effect as we move forward.

Looking a little deeper, we will come across the issue of free will, which is the will not be governed by reason and the individual freedom to choose; still, regardless of whether we can act as we please, we must be upright, careful and respectful in each of our actions, for our benefit, and out of respect for our creator.

But we have been blinded, we have a wrong force that is driving us to act in the wrong way. Sometimes with momentary and seemingly joyful results. These actions deteriorate the soul of each one of the men who live empty without a clear north or purpose, which allows them to see beyond the material and artificial things that surround us.

Precisely, this is the total result that the great seducer and accuser of the world (the Devil) will bring about before his end.

But **the word of God is very clear and is a weapon for spiritual ignorance** and to give understanding to both rulers and beggars, for *God himself said*:

"...my word is truth."

...While the wise King *Solomon*, for his part, wrote:

"that the word of God is wisdom to the soul..."

We are bound by an imperceptible net that uses us as it pleases, where immorality, depravity, and debauchery are seen even in the most inhospitable places in the world, and even in the most inappropriate moments of our leisure time.

We see the greatest stupidities being promoted, gaining ratings and worldwide fame in all mass media. Thus, while foolishness and wickedness among us grow every day, goodness, charity, good deeds, and good acting diminish. Such a situation leads us to be worse than all the wild animals created in nature, this being extremely derogatory for us.

In this regard, *the Bible says in Genesis*:

"So God created mankind in his own image, in the image of God he created them; male and female he created them. God blessed them and said to them, "Be fruitful and increase in number; fill the earth and subdue it. Rule over the fish in the sea and the birds in the sky and over every living creature that moves on the ground."

All these creatures would be under our dominion, for this is one of the conditions that makes us similar to our creator. But this impels us to strengthen our position in the world as people, even though we have been losing this condition... Nevertheless, if we place ourselves under the shadow of the great mantle of our creator and allow his guidance, we will never prevail, for we were made in his image and likeness, created out of love and with perfection, which is the beginning and end, our true center.

For all these reasons, we must awaken from this unreal dream of our so-called reality that is painted as 'life today'.

Even after this generation thought that in the year 2000 the world would end or there would be a catastrophe, today we are still waiting for something better? We must wisely take advantage of the innovations that arise every day, we must surrender our talents to the direction and devotion of the One who provided them to us, we must be diligent in our work, not beating the wind, acting with passion but with prudence, never focusing our priority on goods, money, speed or personal gain, but on how much it will cost me and I will sacrifice of mine to gain of his; how much I will gain for the honor of our God, working for my neighbor as Christ did.

Our mission should be that we may reach a state of spiritual, mental, and physical wholeness, that its result may bring goodness, peace, love, and prosperity in everything, and that we may come closer to the model that Jesus taught us.

Do you know the story of the Hebrew exodus to Canaan? It is very interesting (see Exodus, the second book of the Bible)? And as a well-known evangelist said - it is a real adventure of Faith

Thus, God promised his people in that story:

"Jehovah your God will be with you wherever you go". Then the Word says at the end of Exodus, when they reach the Promised Land: **"and all was fulfilled ..."**

It is worthwhile then also to remember what ***Ellen G. De White*** said:

"those who are at last victorious will have times of terrible perplexity and trials in their spiritual life; but they must not cast away their confidence, for this is a part of their discipline in the school of Christ, and is essential that all dross may be removed."

"The very act in which one renounces one's own life signifies the supreme affirmation of one's personality: it is a return from the periphery to our spiritual center." *- José Ortega & Gasset.*

We are empowered by our Creator to overcome obstacles, break the ego and endure with fortitude any circumstance we have along the way; as long as we keep our center in the direction of the true Light.

The Danger of the Nimble

"Because he himself suffered when he was tempted, he is able to help those who are being tempted." Hebrews 2:18

Our littleness becomes great when we immerse ourselves in the greatness of God.

Sometimes we allow those insignificant and imperceptible things involve us, perhaps they are things that in the eyes of the majority seem even normal and acceptable, but that are not beneficial for us, things that divert us from our objective maturity to walk in wisdom on the right path and under the perfect instructions.

And it is not that this all at once can affect us seriously, it is not a matter of immediate action and reaction, but gradual. Therefore, to let pass what should be corrected without taking action on it and in time will be harmful to anyone.

Those trivial things are all those that are superfluous, those that only satisfy a thought turned into a possible and momentary desire to satiate our 'I' in some way.

On the contrary, everything that pleases God first and is for the benefit of the human beings around us will be shared out of love and charity. Every good example applied and practiced among us with love and righteousness, will be for our own benefit and become part of our blessings.

The wise servant of God of the last century **Ellen G. White** wrote:

"Keep in mind that all who contend for the Faith should do so in a legitimate way, then when they are put to the test they will not be confounded when confronted with their careless claims, nor their word spoken in an impulsive manner."

We have no choice but to take action on all those small and insignificant things around us, and in doing so it is necessary to curb all those that do not offer any gain to our own self and other people.

There is so much imbalance in the world, so much, that it should make the hardest of human hearts weep. There are many people suffering, many falling, hungry, thirsty, sick, disillusioned; others who are clinging, isolated and deranged, but of them, all those who rest best are those who were buried in peace.

Looking away, we see wealthy but greedy and miserable people, unhappy millionaires, famous actors, idols of multitudes who take their own lives, successful people whose spirits have collapsed and who are dead in life.

People without mercy, people trained to serve with excellence in various tasks and who price themselves as if they were inventory items, they look for ways to pile up or simply fill their shelves with more decorative pieces. They are people who have lost even the simplest gesture of appreciation to others, such as an affectionate greeting or a simple "good morning".

We see crimes and breakdowns, along with extreme inequalities in small land divisions of the world, for example, as in the Dominican

Republic and Haiti, as well as in the vast majority of countries on the planet that share the same land.

But there are great human beings, with unimaginable hearts, who have the grace of God, who contribute to their people, their nations, to the world, but who first and foremost contribute to forge and affirm their family nucleus.

There are also people with great ideals of beneficence for humanity, great intellectuals and professionals who use their talents and abilities no matter how, when, and for how much. They strive to do good to this fallen humanity, they are people who take a piece of what they have to give it to someone who asks for it. They represent angelic souls who surround the world to help the needy, they are humanitarians, martyrs who have given and will give their lives for their fellow man.

It is us, those who live in this era of technology and global connection, who must contribute more, give more, be more balanced and measured, since we are the ones who have handled more information in all history, so we must know how to apply it with wisdom, not like those who have eyes and do not see; not like those who have ears and do not listen; but with attention, focus and discernment to learn and teach in truth what is our essence. To achieve this we need our creator to give us the understanding to walk in the light.

We have broken many physical barriers in this world, yet I have never understood why we have not been able to reach balance and understanding as a human race in its fullness.

When the light of the world passes, all difficulties become privileges, confusion becomes order, as the wisdom of God

emerges from what seemed a failure. The gifts of light and life come to us together.

The Power of Mind

In the magnificence of human creation each individual was given a perfect mind, not only in its structure and functional mechanism, which we are still discovering but also in its infinite capacity for visualization, imagination, and creation.

With the mind, we can conceive all that we long for, in it is marked by our past and present, and through it, we can model, visualize and plan the steps towards our future.

It is in the mind where the greatest battles between good and evil are fought, and where the most important wars between our ego and our will are won.

It is the mind that governs the body and emits thoughts. From our thoughts, we develop and define our actions, which give us the results of our day-to-day life.

Our mind is so powerful that despite all the intensive studies in recent years through neurolinguistic programming (NLP) and the exhaustive analysis of the brain's plasticity, we have practically not even begun to understand its depth.

What we do know is that the mind has an impressive capacity for expansion and renewal. This is what the Apostle Paul speaks of in the New Testament of the Bible when he refers to the mind as something so powerful that it has the power to renew itself in its entirety through the spirit; so that clouded understanding, ignorance, and the darkening of thoughts disappear and the spirit and a new mind is reborn.

Ephesians 4 17-20.

So I tell you this, and insist on it in the Lord, that you must no longer live as the Gentiles do, in the futility of their thinking. They are darkened in their understanding and separated from the life of God because of the ignorance that is in them due to the hardening of their hearts. Having lost all sensitivity, they have given themselves over to sensuality so as to indulge in every kind of impurity, and they are full of greed. That, however, is not the way of life you learned

Ephesians 4:23

To be made new in the attitude of your minds.

The mind is like a radio station, and thoughts are the sounds emitted by that station, which come from the voice of the speakers (authors).

Then a question remains that is worth analyzing and reflecting on its answer:

Who is the author of the thoughts or messages that are sent to us, directed, and then emitted to some receiver?

Everything we are is reflected in our mind long before we can see it on the real plane; thus, the external image of ourselves will depend on the internal one.

All that is inside is outside.

What we visualize of ourselves creates a connection between the conscious mind and the subconscious, and this allows us to develop our habits and actions no matter what kind they are.

When we contribute daily to keeping our mind healthy in its thoughts, learning to channel the positive, filtering out the bad, and striving to change the patterns of our old behaviors, our bad habits, and our negative thoughts, for positive, productive, and life-filled thoughts, we will make our inner selves happy. Then we will be making a radical change from our old mentality to a renewed mind.

In this process let us always remember what the innovator and extraordinary *Ralph W Emerson expressed:*

"The mind celebrates a small triumph every time it formulates a thought."

Likewise, and in conclusion, *James Allen* wrote:

"Invigorating thoughts of strength, confidence, and duty. Inspiring thoughts of a grand, free, untrammeled, unselfish life, are useful bricks from which a substantial temple can be erected, and the construction requires that the old thoughts be torn down and destroyed."

The Light of Humanity

The result of our search will be as exact as the path we take.

I am convinced, as is a large part of the world, that we were created in the image and likeness of a God since every created thing has a creator. **We are the patent of a supreme Being, who has acted from a universal point of view.**

This makes it clear that in some way we have God-like capacities, abilities, and qualities. But, at the same time, we are vulnerable.

Now, the problem is not that we know this, for many of us do, and yet there is no significant change in our lives. The problem is that it is not enough to know it or to follow it, we must believe it, see it and feel it. That is what we call FAITH.

Then, once you have obtained it comes the duty and the desire to practice it...

"Faith without works is dead faith," **said Jesus Christ.**

Even when they seem to be intangible things, they are not. They are simply under a light that is not perceptible to human eyes and will cease until your search concludes in that same light. I assure you that this light, which is the only one we will see shining at the end of the road.

We must finish understanding, once and for all, that we are all brothers and sisters, that we must love one another; that we are under the same roof (the world) and the same natural system. That we breathe the same air, and at the end that gives us the family resemblance that we feel and see among us.

Once you understand this, your spirit will have a little more peace. Actions of kindness will come from within you, and the sense of caring for others will come organically. We will not have worries understood as priorities in our lives, but God will put people by your side for you to bring happiness and sacrifice for them.

As long as you practice and reflect regularly, you will be able to convert this routine into a habit, and this habit will bring you so many blessings that your will lead you to climb the rungs of the ladder of success. In this way, your person will be balanced in mind, body, and spirit. You will achieve it in an almost indescribable way, each according to his situation and position.

Let us never think that we are alone. We should not fear anything or anyone, because with this action we could be doubting our faith and relationship with God, in such a case, and according to the word, the only one we should fear is God.

Jesus said, "Do not fear those who kill the body..."

Some may ask: If God is love, why should we fear Him then? But beware, it is not fear of Him, but of disrespecting His will.

I will give a simple example with which I think we will understand much better what I mean:

We all know that the only reason we ran or feared our parents during childhood, was when we did something that although it was an unconscious action of a child, inside we knew was wrong.

That is the fear that the word refers to. So, in the end, it is not He who terrifies us, we terrify ourselves by our actions in the eyes of the living God in the universe, who is our Father.

In the same way, it is our spirit that turns away from the light, because God is love and that light of love always remains fixed in the same place.

Let us look at the great example of the sun. It is the ultimate light of the universe and everything revolves around it; yet, it never moves, it never goes out, and it emits its light unconditionally for all.

There is a profound lesson on this subject, on which we should all reflect.

Try to look gently into the eyes of others and you will see the feeling it brings to repeat this action.

Christ said*: "The eyes are the light of the body".*

You will realize the need for love within yourself and others... Greet, use positive and simple words such as "thank you, please excuse me". Create an atmosphere of love and encouragement around you regardless of your situation. Give it a try.

Jesus was a great Teacher of love. "Man of sorrows," says the word. And I add: - with a mastery of suffering.

He walked through the world as a human to give us a great example of the right path to walk and to explain to us by his walk how our steps should be to be in the light.

Rest, have faith, and take action

We all have a will, even the most fearful; but it is at our point of inability that through the model of Christ, God polishes our faith.

At some point in our lives we have asked ourselves this question:

Now, who am I going to be?

When you have everything on your side, when there are no more resources, no more strength, no more help from others, no more ways out, no more strategies: rest, be alert, and be prayerful.

Almost all of us are incapable of allowing ourselves with a sincere heart to trust and rest in God. However, we understand that even resting in Him we must toil, plan and re-plan, over and over again, often even ignoring God, which is counterproductive.

But the one to whom we owe honor and respect above all else is our Creator, because He loves us so much, that even in these days He continues to give us the special and individual spirit, with talents and virtues each of us, so that in the end we confidently know that He knows the exact point at which we should use our capacities and abilities as human beings.

Just as the apostles had to polish their character and rest totally in Christ to reach fullness, so this would be our example, for all the centuries until the world ceases to be a world.

We must put into practice, *as Jesus said*:

"...rest in Him".

But to achieve this we must make a heartfelt commitment, which is to 'bear His yoke'. Yet He promises that His burden is light and that it is easy to bear the yoke.

So: is it possible to rest while carrying a yoke?

We must learn from Him to understand Him. This is an essential reason for His existence. We have to learn from His behavior, from the attitude and aptitude in His human life, from how He walked in good times and bad, how He spoke, and what He thought.

This has been applied since its origin as the most loved, tested, and sought-after method of rest in all history: God's method of rest.

The Bible defines it in several ways:

"Can any one of you by worrying add a single hour to your life?

*And why do you worry about clothes? See how the flowers of the field grow. They do not labor or spin. Yet I tell you that not even Solomon in all his splendor was dressed like one of these. If that is how God clothes the grass of the field, which is here today and tomorrow is thrown into the fire, will he not much more clothe you— you of little faith?" **Matthew 6: 27-30.***

Further on he goes on to say something even more shocking:

"But seek first his kingdom and his righteousness, and all these things will be given to you as well.[34] Therefore do not worry about tomorrow, for tomorrow will worry about itself. Each day has enough trouble of its own."

Then he makes an incredible confirmation of the truth issued, when he goes on to say, **Matthew 7:**

"Therefore everyone who hears these words of mine and puts them into practice is like a wise man who built his house on the rock."

And I ask you: do you know who the house is? On the other hand, do you know who the rock is?

Finally, it is most striking when **Jesus says**,

"Come to me, all you who labor and are heavy laden, and I will give you rest." **Matthew 11:28.**

Then He explains just how it was that we began the journey to accomplish all this. And He continues:

... "Take my yoke upon you and learn from me, for I am gentle and humble in heart, and you will find rest for your souls. [30] For my yoke is easy and my burden is light.

This does not imply immobility, of course, for even if you are imprisoned, you can always move forward proactively; but you must know yourself and know the model of Jesus. Learning is fundamental for the mind, but as **Dr. Martin L. King** said:

"If you can't fly, run, if you can't run, walk, if you can't walk crawl, but whatever you don't stop moving."

When we analyze these views we observe that it all concludes that although we must possess a firm and virtuous faith, we must at the same time wear the yoke of Christ as a sign of our new character.

The will of God will never permit us to be immovable in our entirety unless it is not for a determined end; on the contrary, it will always permit us to be able to seek the way, within our limited intelligence as mortal beings, to go forward, and never to stop.

With your eyes on the light, keeping your focus, you will never fail to see the path of truth.

We may go as far as our capacities die, as far as our minds explode, as far as our bodies fall, as far as our hearts fail, but the spirit will never faint if it is connected to the divine source.

Confusion inside us

"For what I do, I do not understand; for I do not do what I want, but what I hate, that I do. And if what I do not want, this I do, I approve that the law is good.... So then, when I would do good, I find this law: that evil is in me. For according to the inward man I delight in the law of God. **Romans 7;15,16-21,22.**

In this writing of Paul to the Romans, he explains at length and in-depth the difference between the flesh and the spirit in men; he also explains the influence that the world and the genetic sin we bring with us, humans in flesh and spirit, exert on us, the world and the genetic sin we bring.

Stop physically and mentally at this moment, just for a few minutes...

Feel free to see if you can understand with the spirit and make your sincere inner analysis, if you understand what you are doing, why you are doing it, how you are doing it when you will do it, what will be the result of what you are doing and what, who and why did they induce you to do it?

Mentally associate this with work, your projects, family, friends, achievements, goals, successes, or failures.

Then become aware of the role that the spiritual part plays in order of importance in the things you have been thinking about.

For Paul, as well as for many wise men, thinkers, scientists, astronomers, history makers, and millions of people in the world; the priorities of every human being are, in their respective order, the following:

GOD / You / Marriage / Family / Work / The rest.

We are human and with natural desires, and I understand that; we want food, health, intimacy, financial security, emotional security, etc.; but we often exceed our natural desires no matter how simple they may seem. Any member of our body can lead us to sin.

Paul warns the Romans in his letter not to let any part of their body be inclined to evil, but to use it to do what is pleasing in the sight of our God and Creator.

We all have relapses and difficulties in the process, but thanks to Jesus we are forgiven. Therefore, with our effort and looking to God we can sculpt our being, soul, and body with each fall to try to reach the excellence of Christ.

Then we will see the light, one that was not there before or at least was imperceptible to our eyes. And once we are in the light, we can be lamps that will light others and we can pierce those rays through the dark clouds that threaten our lives and the lives of others.

Feel Imprisoned

Even if your soul no longer fits in with the world, the consistency of your will must support you.

My soul no longer fits in this world, that's why I feel imprisoned.

This is how I have seen it felt and expressed by millions of people on earth, for many reasons.

We all carry an injection of sin in our veins. But this condition is not unalterable, on the contrary, when we understand what differentiates us from other living beings when we understand where we come from, who we are, and where we are going; it is in that empirical process and that knowledge in polishing given only by time, when we learn that life is about something else; and it is when we understand that there is a root from which we descend.

On the other hand, God forgives us for our ignorance. That is to say when we are children we are always in God. In this regard, *Jesus said well*:

"Let the little children come to me, and do not hinder them, for the kingdom of heaven belongs to such as these."

And then, in the same text of the Bible, he adds that all those who want to enter the Kingdom of Heaven must have the soul, the will, and the purity of a child, even when they are adults.

Why does Jesus say this?

It is simple, if you fix your attention, for example, on a child less than 5 years old that you show him a fish or a dead animal in the supermarket, and you tell him that this is to be cooked and eaten, I am almost sure that the answer will always be, "Daddy that is not to be eaten, that is a fish...!" The child will not be able to assimilate because of his nature and naivety about what is happening, and even more, he does not know that already in a few years human conditioning will make it become something normal for him.

This explains the purity of a child's soul. In the end, we all went through that stage, a time when we were a blank book.

The problem lies in the fact that every child who grows up and reaches adulthood forms a personality, a mentality, and spirituality, which does not come in an integrated manual of teachings, but rather, it is a book with pages full of letters written by other hands.

That is why we often feel a lack of belonging to the world, regardless of our jobs, positions, and lifestyles. We feel envy, resentment, quarrels, and everything that overwhelms the world because this situation is the product of all the pages written in our history as human beings.

But, at the same time, we will be the hands that will write on other blank books.

Therefore, we must strive to be the best person we can be and do from the depths of our being everything in our hands to be able to

rewrite the pages that perhaps unintentionally were poorly written in our past.

Then comes the question: How do we make it happen?

Through the Holy Spirit given by God, we will receive everything we need to change these pages that we want to transform in our life.

But we must understand that it is a painful process and unknown to human intelligence because its purpose is to erase from our essence every unusable page full of sin.

In the end, the book will be so perfectly written, that when we rest in our last days as human beings, we know that the one who wrote and perfected the new pages of our lives already has a second part in mind and its continuity will never end.

We must yield a little in this world of so much pressure and speed. We must focus our forces, actions, and prayers on the fundamental and essential causes of our existence, which we must know and respect, without thinking at every moment in an egocentric way, trying to be beings detached from everything that is unimportant and what is superfluous.

In the same way, it happens with the soul, because we take our bodies and minds to an unbridled rhythm, and while we are wrapped in these dark mists that cloud the true light, we cannot see clearly whose hand is writing on us; therefore, we do not want to open the door, so our interior cannot be cleaned.

It is important to understand that there must be a space through which the old and rotten can come out, and the new and refreshing can enter, which will be essential to be in the presence of the spirit of God.

"Look, the Lamb of God, who takes away the sin of the world!"
John 1:29.

Only through Christ can the moral law be kept. In this respect the wise **Ellen G. White** said:

"To have transgressed that law, was what led us to bring sin into the world; and that sin brought with it death, which in the beginnings of the world, did not yet exist for us."

Let us remember what happened to Adam: after having sinned, we see that his first sacrifice with a living being (an animal) was painful; he had to kill an animal, and for the first time he would take the life of a living being; a life that only God could give or restore.

All this is still happening today after many thousands of years have passed. We must become aware, using the opportunities and all the advantages of our era, to change our attitude towards life and to be able to have the grace and favor of God to travel with peace, love, and faith the path that corresponds to us, and consequently, to be an example for the world, society, our environment, and our families.

Once this is achieved, we will be truly complete people and our soul will be elevated by the angels, to see from above the result of the work done here on Earth.

The Bible says in *Isaiah 61:1-2*.

"The Spirit of the Sovereign Lord is on me because the Lord has anointed me to proclaim good news to the poor. He has sent me to bind up the brokenhearted, to proclaim freedom for the captives and release from darkness for the prisoners, to proclaim the year of the Lord's favor and the day of vengeance of our God, to comfort all who mourn..."

As we walk uprightly in the world, even if there are great storms and afflictions on the outside, we will always find peace on the inside; and if we ask for it, God will be with us.

Unity is Strength

"Be completely humble and gentle; be patient, bearing with one another in love. Make every effort to keep the unity of the Spirit through the bond of peace..." **Ephesians 4**

The world is a single image made in the likeness of God, and we are the pieces that make it up.

In some way we all feel, see, think, interpret, communicate and interact. Many of these things we do necessarily and unconsciously as if they were codes injected deep into our DNA, or, simply, as a source of invisible energy that moves us all into balance.

However, we have become so indifferent to our reality that we only see the bubble that we believe to be our environment, a bubble that goes practically against the laws of nature and the balance given by our creator to the entire human race; a bubble that increasingly clouds our perception and drags us to a wrong path in this labyrinth of life.

We are such special beings, that even if we have a heart of stone, like the great example of the Pharaoh of Egypt in the years of Moses, we will be moved and tears will come out of our eyes like any human being when our weaknesses are touched.

And if we were to speak of weaknesses in detail, we would be like a large group of trained ants walking to and for with no definite purpose.

But our strength and greatness are in unity. When there is union everything is possible, when there is the union we are stronger, when there is the union we are capable and nourished by the strengths and experiences of our neighbor and our own. When we are united, we support each other, because if one falls we all fall; but if one triumphs, all will.

God has given us several examples related to real lives through several generations of the importance of being united. We have examples of movements, groups, peoples, and nations that united have traced new paths under His direction, to be led to unimaginable places and achieve things impossible to the human mind as the fall of the walls of Jericho after the people had walked under the instructions of God and as the Hebrew people to cross walking through the middle of the Sea.

All the wars in the world today are ironically mostly because of the divisions created by religious beliefs. In our unbelief, we have lost our sense of coherence with God and nature, or perhaps we have simply preferred not to give it any importance.

We are incapable of reaching healthy agreements without thinking the worst; while our consultants say it must be so. In these times it is almost impossible to be done a favor without asking for something in return.

It was easier to convince hundreds of people a century ago, than to dialogue without strategy with a man today.

Our nature is beautiful by itself, and if we observe it carefully it can tell us many things in relation to the union.

Try to imagine for a moment the position adopted by Moses, the deliverer of the Hebrews, when the time came for the arrival at the sea. God opened a strait so that about four hundred thousand people could cross.

I call that a small sample of God's power through nature, and through man.

We must allow God to take the course of our lives no matter what religion we belong to. In the end, we are all children of the great I AM, and we are all connected in one way or another.

God sees us all as one person through Jesus Christ and has sent us many messages through the history of special people in his eyes, whom he has patiently polished to execute his mission perfectly.

We are a perfect nucleus of love, but every piece that comes off gets lost and spins inside the bubble of the world for the rest of its days.

But the light of God's love will always give us the choice to remain united, and it will also give us a sufficient demonstration through faith.

Human errors

First, we aggrandize ourselves with an impetuous spirit, then we celebrate our own triumphs, leaving others behind. We dig deep and sink little by little into our own holes.

However, it is mortal to make mistakes and we learn from them. Although later we mature and feel dissatisfied.

During this time, we have more responsibilities, and many times we are accompanied by loneliness. Then a feeling of hostility is formed in us. In these cases, many can accumulate evil within themselves, creating a sad atmosphere of individuality, which causes a loss of focus, control, and loyalty.

In spite of everything we are strong, even though we are attacked we are brave, for we were created by a true God. For this reason, we must keep in mind that it is through the Holy Spirit that change is promoted.

As we mature, we begin to see the mistakes, many of them are horrors or bitter tastelessness, they are tests, sometimes long in time, passing, and even simple; in the end, it does not matter how they are, the goal is to resist in any way.

In the next step will come the test of true Faith, the Faith that is sincere and sure of what it expects; the Faith that can do everything, the Faith that is born of love; the Faith that illuminates your virtues, the Faith that eliminates all error, the Faith that renews the fountains of your house so that you may drink fresh water and rest your clamor, and that the desperate and anxious song may become peace and devotion.

We tend to hide when we make mistakes, but it is the bad ones who run; the good ones resist what God put inside their hearts.

Resistance gives strength, as our past mistakes heal, fears are lost, then grass and flowers grow in the wasteland that hides the depths of our ambitions.

Strong and virile must be our posture in the face of challenges in moments of bitterness: when that white cloud clouds over, when you feel that God is leaving and that for an instant you are alone and without help, when you think you are falling, when you feel confused as you walk, just for the simple fact of not trusting.

At the end of the road, there will always be hope, as long as there is a teacher there will be teachings; as long as there are dreamers there will be dreams and people who live them, who make them come true and pursue them.

So do not be afraid to correct your mistakes, cleanse your heart and begin to heal other hearts; go walking quietly confident that Christ is alive. With genuine faith, my brother! That is what I call greatness with humility and style.

Finally, when we know the lives of so many martyrs and other men who have fought steadfastly and died for their conviction of the truth, we must at least ponder in our thoughts:

What is it that is so Great that makes a human being such a faithful servant, that his life is laid before the cause he loves, with his head held high, his spirit at peace and his heart lifted up?

Luke 16:10

"Whoever can be trusted with very little can also be trusted with much, and whoever is dishonest with very little will also be dishonest with much."

2 Timothy 2:15:

"Do your best to present yourself to God as one approved, a worker who does not need to be ashamed and who correctly handles the word of truth."

Brave Mind and Sincere Heart

When mind and heart are united in the same ideal and focus, the force of passion and vigorous spirit give the being its full potential and assume its real position in the world to fulfill its destiny.

"To educate the mind without educating the heart; is not to educate at all." **Aristotle**.

In this time we need more brave minds, minds that have the same level of preparation and physical strength that the leaders and leaders of the great ancient peoples and armies possessed.

We well know that nowadays war in its maximum expression is mental and spiritual, that is to say, it happens within us. We could say, without fear of being wrong, that we are living in the most prolific century in history, but also the most dangerous and vulnerable.

The more mastery we have over ourselves in a fully connected world, the better our future will be. It is we who determine the level of discipline we will tolerate and what will be the high points of surrender in our journey.

The fatalities that poison the inner man are at the click of a button, put on a menu at the request and choice of the general public: no filters,

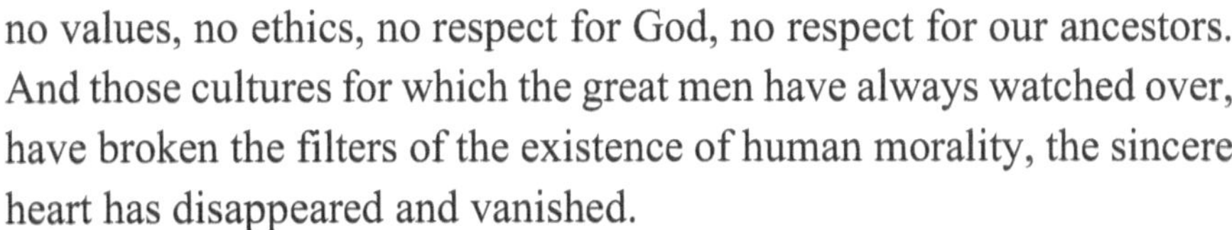

no values, no ethics, no respect for God, no respect for our ancestors. And those cultures for which the great men have always watched over, have broken the filters of the existence of human morality, the sincere heart has disappeared and vanished.

But there is a preventive formula which enables us to strengthen our mind to a point inconceivable before our own experience, and which will put in our heart a genuine sincerity and a proven humility.

The formula is this:

"Be careful not to practice your righteousness in front of others to be seen by them. If you do, you will have no reward from your Father in heaven. So when you give to the needy, do not announce it with trumpets, as the hypocrites do in the synagogues and on the streets, to be honored by others. Truly I tell you, they have received their reward in full. But when you give to the needy, do not let your left hand know what your right hand is doing, so that your giving may be in secret." **Matthew 6.**

These Bible verses explain very clearly what function a heart must exercise to find its balance and sincerity, once it has entered into the process of cleansing itself of all self-importance and self-sufficiency.

And we see that what comes from self-complacency, in every sense of the word, takes away our confidence before God; and therefore, the communicative channels of the spirit cut their link, just as it happens in a couple's relationship when communication ends: affinity is cut off and, consequently, the bond deteriorates, until the loving yoke is broken.

On the other hand, there is the best part... and it is the one referred to in **Jesus'** teaching:

"Whatever you ask for in prayer, believe that you have received it, and it will be yours."

This sounds like a movie script, but it has already been tested by hundreds of thousands of people, and it is the most powerful formula to ensure the strengthening of our mind; perhaps it is a very simple prayer, but its content carries a level of depth that I would have to use several pages to describe in a subtle way the whole context.

However, from my point of view, this is an apt explanation that follows from **Deepack Chopra's** analysis, when he spoke about the words spoken by Jesus:

Perhaps it is the simplest expression of a teaching repeated by Jesus frequently. You must have faith... So for centuries prayer has had a hidden component: a litmus test for Faith. It is difficult to pray without feeling a pang of guilt and doubt.

Do I have enough faith, and what am I doing wrong that my prayers are not being answered? Obeying this command depends on the level of consciousness. At the lower levels, one asks for help.

At the higher levels, a prayer is no different from any other thought, because every thought has a result.

In between are all kinds of possibilities. Jesus undoubtedly knew all that, so he asks us to believe that our prayers will come true."

This is a valuable teaching at any level of consciousness. He takes it for granted that Jesus is telling the truth and that prayer will be answered.

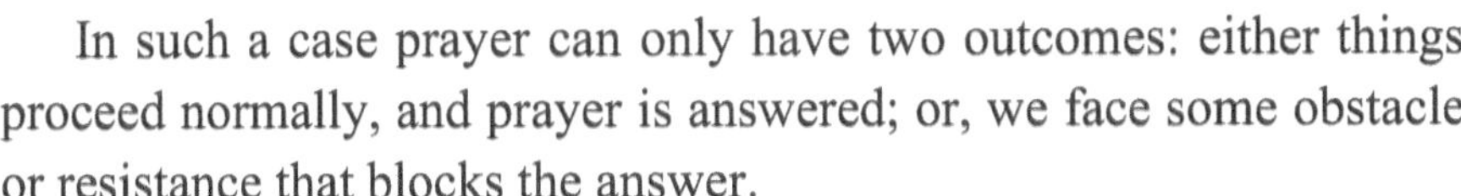

In such a case prayer can only have two outcomes: either things proceed normally, and prayer is answered; or, we face some obstacle or resistance that blocks the answer.

Obstacles and resistance exist in the consciousness and can therefore be removed.

Rather than being a litmus test for Faith, prayer teaches us that what we must do on the spiritual path is to open the channels of communication. The help Jesus offers us is to ensure that communication is never interrupted, only temporarily blocked.

The mind will be our direct link, and to keep its functioning in a positive way in a pure state, as our master walked, all your capacity will be available for its strengthening.

At the end of the process, we will be new human beings, with sincere hearts, a strong and willing mind, who will put all our capabilities to contribute productive things to society, and become a channel of light for the glory of our God.

To be born, to grow, and to know

> *Blessed is he who dies and is born again every day, for at the coming of the darkness of the day he shall die; but at every rising of the sun, he shall shine forth as a new man bringing light into the world and strengthening his roots from the sap of the earth where he was buried, there where only true men are born again.*

Since the questions lead us to question and internal analysis, I would like to start with these questions:

- ➢ How can we know how well we are doing?

- ➢ How right are we acting?

- ➢ What is the moral gravity of our behavior?

- ➢ What results do we envision in our future: will I have a family, children, a great company?

- ➢ What will the next generation do?

To obtain answers with a reflective point, and to achieve a good result that allows us to put it into practice, let us analyze the following: how since the times of Socrates, before Christ, we see that the practice applied by all the great masters, and even by the greatest and most transcendental of all, Jesus Christ, is: know thyself...

In this regard the Apostle Paul wrote in his second letter to the Corinthians:

"Examine yourselves, to see whether you are in the Faith; test yourselves, or do you not know yourselves?"

And he ends by asking everyone regardless of how long they have known Him, or whether they have heard of Him:

"Do you not know that Christ is in you?".

As we see, as many scholars explain in this writing on the word of God, the Apostle Paul expresses very clearly his focus on what should be the central axis and point of reflection in this whole matter:

1st observation: he says to examine ourselves. We must examine ourselves with the purity of the truth, so as not to be disqualified in trying to teach others.

More important is to know that if there is not full confidence in that which we hope for, but cannot see, we will never see it; for, our faith is not virtuous, nor our obedience confident. But once you understand who it is that leads, then you will be on the way to achieving it.

2nd observation: as Paul well expressed: "Prove yourselves"; we must prove ourselves, and this implies much: it implies the courage to take it on, honesty to do it correctly, patience to endure during the wait, wisdom to resist the defect of our short-inherited intelligence, and love to demonstrate after all that you correspond to those who run the race for the truth.

This step entails trials and they perfect our character, giving luster to our true morals.

The tests are the prelude to the diploma of commemoration that will give us the power to teach others all that we have learned in our journey.

This scope may be a light placed on a high place so that many may see through it.

The tests correspond to the acquisition of the patience you will need in the future to be able to bear with love and calm, the burden that comes with the level of responsibility that comes with everything you ask God every day.

If after you have passed these tests and you deviate your course from the final lick, remember that even so, we still have God's grace.

<u>3rd observation</u>: know ourselves. Finally, to know ourselves is perhaps a long and for many a never-ending task.

This reflection will lead us to remember the time of the great philosopher Socrates, who is one of his aphorisms said:

"know thyself".

That was almost 400 years before the coming of Christ into the world, as the son of God, who also said: *"Love one another as I have loved you"*.

Clearly for this to be literal, we must know ourselves. This is so clear that God then lays down the commandments, and one of them reads:

"you shall love your neighbor as yourself."

To achieve this, we must know ourselves. And the fruit of this will be our transfer and knowledge to others, as a sign of love for our neighbor, recognizing our equality as children of a single father and creator of the universe, who is God.

If every day we try to dominate ourselves and look more to the example of Christ. If we put our trust in a true God who has guided and perfected through these methods hundreds of his saints, will he not be able to do so with us as well?

But in the end, that is our great choice. So, no matter what comes: which will be the path of your walk: God's or the world's?

A Brilliant Character

"Have mercy on me, O God, according to your unfailing love; according to your great compassion blot out my transgressions." **Psalm 51.**

We are inconsistent in our education, disposition, and integrity. We do not understand what the journey is about because we only see the surroundings. We cannot bear to take the necessary steps, we give up in the face of the trials we must face and resist, and we do not even endure the time that is necessary to achieve what we know we must achieve; simply because we are not educated for it.

We are blind under a system of modernism that does not allow us to discern, understand and evaluate the true reason for our existence as human beings; for this reason, many of us die without ever understanding the meaning of life; millions of us die empty in our deepest existence, and others carve a path that in the end brings them disappointment and sadness, allowing themselves to be dragged down by previous joys.

Many, who have the talent to be able to act, want to gain a reputation in stupid and degrading ways. They are blinded by ignorance without any understanding that true reputation is obtained from desire and passion born of the virtue of action.

Philip Stanhope, 4th Earl of Chesterfield, statesman, and man of letters, said:

"character must be kept clean and bright."

I have come to visualize our next generations as beings accommodated to a fictitious, dull, corrupt, and confusing system, living in a world covered by imbalance and loss of values and morals, cataloging with human judgments the right and wrong, completely obviating the true law of justice and balance, the only perfect one, not traced by human hands, nor thought by limited mind, but by the infinite wisdom of our Creator.

We are spiritual beings and therefore the real connections will always be imperceptible to the eyes of men, but the results of obedience will give such a concrete and satisfactory answer to the believer, that he will be light to the world and his testimony will be comfortable and rest to many who have insatiable emptiness, incorrigible frustrations, weary spirits, and inconsolable sorrows.

As we tell others about our experiences, we will strengthen our spirit with the truth. And as the word says: *"...and the truth shall set you free."*

Our actions can be executed by our body and mind, without God's consent, which is clearly why we have free will. Now, we must evaluate the consequences of our actions, for, by it, we will be judged.

As it says in ***Proverbs***, written by the wise of the wise, King Solomon, son of David, in ***Chapter 2 verse.1:***

"My son, if you accept my words and store up my commands within you, turning your ear to wisdom and applying your heart to understanding— indeed, if you call out for insight and cry aloud for understanding, and if you look for it as for silver and search for it as for hidden treasure, then you will understand the fear of the Lord and find the knowledge of God. For the Lord gives wisdom; from his mouth come knowledge and understanding. He holds success in store for the upright, he is a shield to those whose walk is blameless, for he guards the course of the just and protects the way of his faithful ones.

Then you will understand what is right and just and fair—every good path. For wisdom will enter your heart, and knowledge will be pleasant to your soul. Discretion will protect you, and understanding will guard you.

Wisdom will save you from the ways of wicked men, from men whose words are perverse, who have left the straight paths to walk in dark ways."

Let us remember that we live for a limited time and that we must give our best for our world and leave seeds sown that can grow tall, under God's will.

As **B. Gracian** said:

"What fortune has of inconstant, fame has of the firm. The former is for living; the latter is for later. The former is besieged by envy, the latter is threatened by oblivion. Fortune is desired, while fame is obtained by one's efforts. Fame is the sister of giants, it always moves in extremes... monsters or prodigies, rejections or applause."

The inner change process

Everything starts from within, there will never be a change in our life without first having conquered our inner self.

I believe God has called many of us to put our talents to His will.

Many of us have struggled internally with things we don't know. We suffer too much, to the point of sometimes forgetting to laugh, and it may be that our soul perhaps feels like the biceps of the body in its early days when we usually exercise. Then we feel relief and our soul, like those biceps, calms down, relaxes, is fortified, its consistency is now more solid and it constantly seeks the higher spirit (the Holy Spirit). Sometimes we lose sight of Him, but He remains there, if we kneel and look for Him again He will make Himself felt.

In the same way, we feel that everything that are not sincere, pure, genuine words, and that come from love, are rejected by our soul; at the same time an anger is born in us for the evil we see and that feeling constantly stirs our consciences, observing people and seeing calamity in the circle that embroils us: it is here that we begin to grow inwardly.

At one moment you may think that these issues are flashes of the inner brokenness you have experienced; then a feeling of duty and a restlessness to sow and cultivate good words and actions in the depths of your people, your environment, or your nation begins to creep into your soul.

In this process, the time will come when you will feel the blockage of everything: probably you will not be able to use your abilities and talents in other tasks; and you will want to blow up that wall, but you will not be able to, because it will be part of the stage in which you are.

Then you will do nothing but think in a thousand ways about immediate action, but at that moment you must find calmness and remember that "Wisdom thinks calmly; what diligence executes quickly".

When you go through this type of inner process, it will generally awaken in you a desire to seek God and it is when a new mentality begins to be reborn. For this reason, you will see in your mind, talents, will, feelings and inner being, like a carpet for the Lord to step on them and leave his stamp engraved on you completely, and thus many will be revived and revived through you.

Let us be founders, each one individually and in our environment, as an entity full of strength and light, to give to others.

Let us embark with fortitude on the path of truth without letting any human suggestion make us change our minds. We are the protagonists of our destiny, and the director stares at us through the eye of the camera in the sky, waiting for the excellent action of the talents given to us from the work of his creation.

Let us be sowers of values, respect, and love; this does not imply a lack of character, righteousness, and courage, on the contrary, it will give to the heart of each one of us the special armor of the Spirit. From

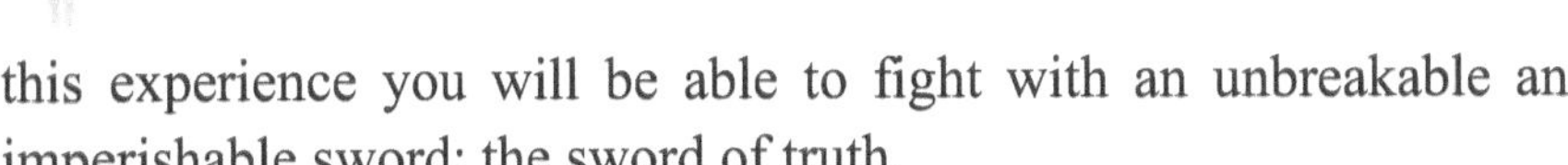

this experience you will be able to fight with an unbreakable and imperishable sword: the sword of truth.

So how will we know when we will be ready to exercise our function excellently?

We will be ready when the chains of virtues that complement us as human beings are perfected, and we reach serenity.

Virtue leads a man to acquire wisdom, integrity, moderation, courage and as a result the true applause of a courageous man. Virtue is so beautiful that it brings God's contentment, and makes us the light of all the people around us.

Great men are measured by virtue and so are loved when they live and remembered after their death. Even, for some, because of their great virtues and proofs of courage and Faith, God has exonerated them from death; let us look at the example of Elijah.

A great man once said, *"Three axes bring bliss: Holy, Healthy, and Wise."*

Virtue is the sun of the world called a man and the hemisphere is the good conscience.

We all have defects

Though we are sinners our hearts and minds are endowed with the substance that is within the core of love of our perfect creator.

We have all sinned we are born with sin. It is something that comes in our genes, it is hereditary from shortly after the creation of the human race. We come with the impurity of having disobeyed God's designs, and our acquired guilt is the most dangerous weapon or the most effective healing medicine:

How can this be?

First, we must understand in a general way that to truly move forward in life we must admit our guilt. For that it is necessary to recognize and internalize, and to get inside we must reflect, pray and meditate.

When we achieve this first part we are already winning, because regardless of the circumstances we acquire a position of understanding and relaxation in any situation, trusting in something greater and supreme, which is God.

What comes next is to recognize that some things within us are wrong. At the same time, we must remember that error is not a defect, as it can be due to ignorance as well as recklessness. To be clear, we all have been there or will be there at some point. This is what we call guilt.

That is why, when the Bible recounts the event where Jesus defends an adulterous woman who was to be stoned, it took only one prayer of wisdom that reached right into the spirit of each of the attacking men and broke their hearts, leaving them stunned. He straightened up and said to them:

"He that is without sin among you shall be the first to cast a stone at her."

At that moment everyone was stunned, those who had stones in their hands in a few seconds dropped them, many ran and others were speechless.

Here we discover the human being in his condition as a sinner. The Master shows the power of inner guilt, and how to avoid an inhuman and bloody event when the inner conscience realizes the error.

This special condition, of being able to transform ourselves in such a positive way and drastically change for the better all our mistakes by simply beginning to search ourselves internally, is the result of the knowledge of our spirit and the Spirit of God that nourishes it. It is the legacy of the spiritual experience left by the Son of God as a light lit in the heart of every human being who decides to seek Him.

Finally, we must be aware of the community to which we belong, whose nature is of one race. And we must understand that it is not under laws, regulations, and external human conditions that we must govern ourselves to change our impure condition.

The accusations and denunciations among us have become a destabilizing and alarming element in society. But somehow we must undertake projects that contribute to general change, using God's method, not that of men.

We must rearm society through all possible mass and educational means, we must raise awareness from the inside out as Jesus taught.

We must re-establish and re-stabilize our families, schools, and the media, which are the ones that shape the ideal and the character of each one of us. We must wholeheartedly resolve in our personal and professional lives to serve others, which is the golden rule and leave behind the self-centered pursuit of self.

The New World Chip

> *It is not the world that is our conquest to attain glory; it is attaining glory that is our conquest over the world.*

This world does not have much time left. Let's be honest with ourselves, at this very moment regardless of your position, age, or sex, this world is full of indifference, fear, evil, and as if that were not enough, we are now surrounded by intelligent objects that turn out to be more apparently intelligent than us.

We are rampantly rushing around, killing our body and spirit to get things we don't need, that only serve to impress people who ultimately don't care about us and persuasively force us to spend money we don't even have. And if some of you manage to obtain these objects by acting under these standards, then you are doubly mistaken.

We have enveloped ourselves in a synthetic bubble that is filled with misinformation that is not pleasing to the eye or the soul; with shocking and bewildering images that occur at an enormous speed and cause our eyes to lose sight of reality more and more each day. Just as a single cloud can for a moment eclipse the rays of the sun...

That speed is the essence of the bad seed that is growing among us, that speed does not allow us to reflect.

That speed leads professionals in any field to believe the movie in which the great seducer of the world, Satan, has wrapped us; giving us an overdose of worldliness to try to make us believe that we are the owners of the vineyard when we are only farmers and temporary stewards.

Brethren, God demands of us that we understand once and for all what the truth of the world is. It is necessary to understand that we are only tillers of God's ground and, therefore, our function is to sow the seed and water it under the rules and conditions of nature. It is only God who allows the acorn to grow to the height and width of His will.

Factors such as ignorance, self-sufficiency, self-indulgence, love of material things, idolatry of money, and the need to feel capable in a society blinded by the things of the world, are what are completely deteriorating our countries, communities, and families.

It is the struggle to have and to possess that has intoxicated the culture of such beautiful nations like the United States, Latin America, and the Caribbean, degrading the beloved people of God to lameness itself.

A great sage of the 16th century said:

"The sane man must adapt himself to the present, although it seems to him better the past, both in the clothes of the body, as in those of the soul. It seems a thing of other times, and one does not know how to speak the truth, to keep one's word. Good men seem to have been made in the past, though they are always loved, if there are any, they are not fashionable or esteemed."

We need to be practical people in the world but under the discipline of our inner being. If we are discreet, we should live as we can and without burden.

How common is wickedness in our present times and how strange virtue!

We should prefer what has been granted to us by the grace of God and pray to preserve talents, instead of paying attention to what has been momentarily denied us.

In the Bible, at the time of the Sermon on the Mount, Jesus expresses words of imperishable wisdom that speak clearly of God's providence as a promise to us men as his beloved children made in his image and likeness.

Matthew 6:27-30 says:

Can any one of you by worrying add a single hour to your life? "And why do you worry about clothes? See how the flowers of the field grow. They do not labor or spin. Yet I tell you that not even Solomon in all his splendor was dressed like one of these. If that is how God clothes the grass of the field, which is here today and tomorrow is thrown into the fire, will he not much more clothe you—you of little faith?

Deepack Chopra wrote among his many spiritual books; specifically, one that he dedicated to the study of the figure of Jesus, something that explains in practical terms the Bible verse that speaks of what the expression "God will provide" means.

He writes:

"In the Sermon on the Mount Jesus offers an idea so simple and revolutionary that it changes everything we assume to be existence. This is the idea: "Let God take care of everything".

In this verse, the most basic needs, food, and clothing are left in God's hands. But Jesus knew that making clothes requires work, so what did he mean when he proclaimed that God would provide?

The crux of the matter is freedom. Free from hard work, worry, and suffering, we find that nature provides everything.

We generally think of ourselves as complex creatures, the opposite of lilies of the field, because our existence depends on effort.

For Jesus, this is a mistake. Since we are more like God in our ability to be conscious, God provides for us to a greater extent than plants and animals. But he does not do so in the same way. Having consciousness, we receive our sustenance through the mind. The physical world comes from the mind of God, and when we approach Him, all of creation becomes part of us.

The divine glory clothes us. Without Faith, this glory remains hidden from view. We believe that the world is separate from us and that it is generally hostile to our needs. It becomes necessary for Jesus, in his superior state of consciousness, to show us an approach that frees us from this limited perception. Once liberated, we enjoy the glory like the lilies of the field.

Marriage, Love, and Commitment

Some Pharisees came to him to test him. They asked, "Is it lawful for a man to divorce his wife for any and every reason?" "Haven't you read, he replied, that at the beginning the Creator 'made them male and female,' and said, 'For this reason, a man will leave his father and mother and be united to his wife, and the two will become one flesh? So they are no longer two, but one flesh.' Therefore what God has joined together, let no one separate." Matthew 19:3-6

Marriage can be a well-grounded nest of love, it can be a confusing and merciless abyss, it can be a pause in your life or a lifetime in a union without pause. Marriage can have a happy ending, or it can be a total catastrophe; it can be a seed that grows strong and bears fruit or an oak uprooted at the wrong time; it can be a sweet transitory teaching, as well as an unrepeatable bitter pill.

In a world where we inhabit more than seven billion human beings and where approximately one million eight hundred thousand babies are born every week, all men and women, it is indisputable that marriage can develop in multiple ways and have innumerable results.

Even so, the Bible tells us how we should walk and what we should do to obtain the right outcome of love and well-being.

The key is within us; it is we who determine the direction and the continuing course our relationship takes; it is we who choose our partners; look at Shakespeare as he died for love; look at Samson, the man with the most physical strength in history as he loses his strength to his beloved.

Every human being on Earth cries out for love. True love within a marriage will transcend any physical, mental or spiritual barrier that exists in our lives, yet just as important as love is commitment.

For some reason, people change when they love, and I am not talking about feeling in love because falling in love is something fleeting. I am talking about the change in our face, our look, our vision of life, how we see things, our spirit is moved and we feel our whole body vibrate, as when a vocalist feels his vocal cords when singing his highest melody. Our manners change, there is a glow in us, and most striking of all, problems vanish.

If we are young our vigor grows, our hormones explode; if we are adults we are rejuvenated and all that lost strength and charisma we thought we had lost or forgotten comes back.

This is our base to be able to start sowing in fertile ground. Know that no matter how you look at it, if there is no love and commitment in the union between two people, its result will be perishable and its journey unsatisfactory.

Some of us, as Christ said, are not born to be able to receive this experience. Similarly, the Bible states that only fornication or adultery could result in a legal rupture, although this act is still an offense in the eyes of God. Then He said to them, "Not all can receive this, but those to whom it is given."

In the famous novel of a century, ago called Anna Karenina, by Leo Tolstoy, we are told that the charismatic, beautiful, and intelligent protagonist of high society who, supposedly in the eyes of the people led a perfect marriage and family life, has a husband of a man of high rank and a son whom she loves; she leads a balanced social life among her friends and family. Although Ana's married life was pleasant, everything fell apart when an elegant and handsome officer appeared and unleashed her emotions and passions that she had never felt with her husband. Ana and the elegant officer will start a love affair, and everyone finds out, but this will cost her family and reputation.

Then the relationship begins to deteriorate. Ana is left on the brink of ruin, alone and ashamed...

The key is in us; for, if we can conquer someone to be our eternal partner, we should also be able to choose, and even more so to keep it.

But something always happens to us in the process, something with our thoughts, our flesh, our devotion to the other person, and we begin to say that love is gone; or, perhaps, it just never was.

Shakespeare talks about lust in an interesting way. In many of his plays he denotes the conflict between the passions and reason, which must be united in an organic love for there to be understanding:

"Waste of spirit in shame lust is in act and up to the act perjured, bloodthirsty, treacherous, savage, extreme, cruel and harsh. It is despised as soon as it is enjoyed, longed for without measure, and once it is achieved, hated without measure, like a bait that unnerves the unwary who swallows it".

Marriage must bring with it an exceptional personal effort, determinant and with a strict discipline; for, we are weak in the flesh and sexuality, and the current erotic pleasures do not let us live: we are overwhelmed by obscene advertisements, physical and virtual prostitution, moral disinformation, love for the body and its perfection, and we leave behind the spirit, the mind and the soul, which is the essence of us as human beings.

But if we apply the right steps to our relationship, we can achieve what for many seems like a dream that will never be achieved:

And these would be the steps to follow:

> Love is indispensable in a relationship, without it we will never be one flesh, it will always be two.

> Personal communication is what unites our souls, if we lose communication, the links break.

> Understanding, knowing how to listen, listen and help our partner.

> Healthy habits between the two, both in the treatment, verbal, sexual, physical, and spiritual.

> Discipline, to be able to withdraw from bad ways, to create ineffable righteousness over time.

The physical touch of our partner and its continued maintenance is important; for this, we must try to be tactful; but calm, even so, we will always want more. Always walk with attention and detail is the key.

Patience, a lot of patience to endure the things that happen and that we do not expect, those disconcerting and insecure moments where our reality is clouded and we are invaded by a passing thought of insecurity or falsehood.

Acts of kindness and service to our partner create a bond of love like that of Jesus Christ, an example that needs no words, deeds that will always remain in our hearts and in the hearts of those we serve.

We must never mix yesterday and today when we continually look back. It could happen to us as it did to Lot's wife. It is as if we were driving a car at full speed and staring in the rearview mirror.

We must always look ahead and united to that bond of love and commitment to the other person we choose to take with us. Surely, despite the ability, we need to walk together with all our lives, it will bring gratification to our souls.

The Meaning of Life

"Whoever pursues righteousness and love finds life, prosperity and honor." **Proverbs 21:21.**

More than existence is our desire to live. That desire makes us endure and adapt to any eventuality in life. If we see it from a non-material plane, we will see that it is not the essence of having that makes us weak in spirit, but the abandonment of what once brought us to where we are, which is the same thing that holds us back.

We are not the ones who determine our essence, it is God who under the fulfillment of his word keeps the whole universe in balance.

It is very interesting to see what the law of adversity indicates to us: we need to stumble for our character to emerge and develop, and we need to persevere in the process of changes to overcome them.

That's to say, we need to receive persistent chiseling from our sculptor, just as a sculpture is perfected when we remove the leftover parts; parts that perhaps we are not born with, but that we attach to us as the years go by, and that at the moment they are removed produce pain; but, we will emerge refined and shining like a diamond after it is finished.

When we look at the lives of the great orators, philosophers, apostles, leaders, and rulers who lived in some historical past, we realize that they were fighters of the Faith, who persisted to the end to defend what they understood gave meaning to their lives, and under that adversity were sowers of seeds so special contained by their passion and dedication; they gave leafy, persistent, large and nourished trees.

On the other hand, we see how many times prosperity, tranquility, and comfort, in general terms, lead us to a comfort zone that makes us indulge our true essence, replacing the real and pure vision of our purpose in life.

Likewise, while our spiritual and mental strength weakens, our carnal strength and devotion to material things grow. Then we demand, complain in a demanding and insulting manner in the eyes of our creator when our true act of spiritual balance and surrender should be to give thanks each day for life and the few or many blessings we have, making every effort to act for others as we would like them to act for us.

Imminent support will come from heaven and fill our souls, activating our senses with the greatness of spirit. So we will be able to give others a token of faith for each day. Our actions and words will emphasize the truth in these times where information is so intense, diverse, and overwhelming, that the most shocking truths already begin to lose interest, and where damaged minds, unbalanced by perversion and vanity, cause thousands of evils in the world.

In this vein, *Leo Tolstoy* wrote:

"Faith is the knowledge of the meaning of human life, a knowledge that causes man not to destroy himself but to live, faith is the force of life."

Let us share what we have, be it little or much, let us give what we know, let us teach and love; and when we put effort into these virtues we will begin to give true meaning to our lives and we will walk safely in the direction of our purpose.

Sensuality and Morality

"For although they knew God, they neither glorified him as God nor gave thanks to him, but their thinking became futile and their foolish hearts were darkened. Although they claimed to be wise, they became fools [23] and exchanged the glory of the immortal God for images made to look like a mortal human being and birds and animals and reptiles.... and because they approved not to regard God, God gave them over to a reprobate mind to do things not fitting; being filled with all unrighteousness, fornication, perverseness, covetousness, wickedness; full of envy, murder, strife, deceit, and malignity...revilers, haughty, inventors of evil, unfaithful, without natural affection..." **Romans 1:21-31.**

This is a Bible verse that may seem very strong and disturbing. I know that it is delicate to talk about these things and much more difficult to let our minds assimilate them without passing any judgment.

But it is also a reality of the uncontrolled pace of life that this last generation is experiencing in the world. It seems to be extreme in all its parts, physically, mentally, and spiritually.

Don't you feel the same when you go out on the street and look around you?

Now, let's go to the main context of this topic, which is ourselves and the way we have lived until today, dragging with carnal chains that spirit of sensuality that we are unable to undo or avoid.

Human passions and sensualities have reached a climax in our generation, not even Sodom and Gomorrah are similar to what we live today: it is an evil that almost all of us have experienced (leaving the benefit of the doubt) because if it is true, in Sodom and Gomorrah before being destroyed by God, only one just man with his family was found in the whole earth; and this man was Lot, only one! of all the inhabitants of the cities, it seems incredible...

Now, let's imagine what will become of us now that we have almost every city in the world connected to internet networks. And let's add to that the pornographic factor and the depravity that has been sown in the last generations of humanity through the screens...

We must internalize and work on self-respect, to try to straighten out the defects of character and bring our person to be able to bind those passions and sensualities that overwhelm us.

It may not matter to many at this time to have depraved thoughts, and others, even, execute wrong actions, such as having sex with anyone who passes them by, practicing uncontrolled masturbation, watching pornography constantly, desiring the men or women they see daily on the networks half-naked, etc.

But I know that many seek how to take care of the mind of what they see, which involves healing the soul and how to direct their spirit on the path of peace and well-being.

Depression, dissatisfaction, and sometimes the existential emptiness we feel, comes from the darkness and dark places we have within us (mind and soul); from sensualities, uncontrolled misaligned passions, whether past or present, that lead us to failure and emotional instability in the essential responsibilities to God, to ourselves and others.

Still, there is good news, words of comfort and hope for us; words with life that have instilled change in hundreds of thousands of people, who have successfully overcome and chained this carnal sensuality that moves us.

Let us look at part of the story of Joseph. A man who, according to Genesis, underwent many very hard human trials since his childhood. Within these trials, he was tempted by sensuality and the passions of the flesh. Such incitement was made by the wife of the one who was at that time his master. She told him to sleep with her and tried to seduce him with her words. But Joseph never yielded. He responded with all his morals and confidence high, and above all concerning disrespect. A pure spirit of respect for God was evident in his actions and words, and his final results were a spectacle to the world.

However dark it may seem that which we still feel or do, which does not give us peace even though it gives us carnal satisfaction; which internally makes a silent noise that is breaking our moral eardrums; even so, we can let in the light, we can change our present course and entrust ourselves to God, trusting in His spirit to heal ours and be bound to His forever.

Paul tells the Philippians:

"Not that I have already obtained all this, or have already arrived at my goal, but I press on to take holdof that for which Christ Jesus took hold of me. [13] Brothers and sisters, I do not consider myself yet to have taken hold of it. But one thing I do: Forgetting what is behind and straining toward what is ahead,[14] I press on toward the goal..."

True love and respect for ourselves and others will bring honor and purity to our soul, home, family, work, and everything around us.

Christ said:

"Blessed are the pure in heart, for they shall see God."

We must let God cleanse our hearts to be able to let in the light that illuminates the soul, for it is necessary to do our part and follow the example of Christ.

However thick the darkness may be, the sun rises for everyone and everything on earth; it rises for both the just and the unjust.

Regardless of which of these groups you are in, go out and cleanse yourself of all vain sensuality that does not allow you to grow within, and seek the light that was made for you.

The Power of Tongue

The tongue is a member that seems insignificant to human eyes, it is soft, moist, and of very little physical attractiveness, unlike other parts of our body.

By definition, the tongue is an organ that contains salivary glands; it is located inside the body, which means that we cannot see it with the naked eye; it is odd, medium-sized, and symmetrical, and performs important functions such as moisturizing the mouth and processing food through salivation; it is involved in language and the sense of taste. Swallowing and speaking are practically impossible without saliva.

Its extraordinary vascularization and other exceptional qualities allow its mobility, making it a very special organ; so much so, that if other muscles of the body had such attributes, we would practically be supermen who would never become exhausted no matter what type of physical activity we practice; in short, we would never get tired.

This perhaps little-heard exposition will bring curiosity to our thoughts, but let us keep the focus on what follows, for if we believe that what is said above makes this organ special, we will be surprised to learn that its so extraordinary qualities could also be the most nefarious if we were to misuse it.

The fact that the tongue is lodged inside the body means that when we look in the mirror we cannot see it unless we intentionally pull it out. This would involve using the brain to induce that part of the body to act as we wish. We would have to do the same to be able to speak, a function that goes beyond the mere use of the referred muscle or organ, because not even we, being masters of our tongue, can control it.

Entering into the context of speech (a quality that differentiates us from other living beings) and the tongue, let us subtract ourselves in this example: the great titanic ships that glide through the waters of the sea and that despite their enormous size, majesty, weight, and firmness, are moved by a small rudder, which is directed by a captain. So, if the rudder is our tongue, there is no doubt that our mind must be the captain.

The most handsome among thousands and the wisest among millions will be rejected by others if he does not know how to control his tongue.

It is not enough to moderate it; it is a matter of taming it to be able to direct it, without losing sight of its objective, for which reason it is necessary to know the function it exercises in our body.

The Bible says:

"For every nature of beasts, and of birds, and of serpents, and of creatures of the sea is tamed, and hath been tamed by human nature."

And it is precisely the tongue the organ that has allowed us, among other things, to name the animals that have existed since God created the world, for it was a predestined blessing for us to dominate the Earth and have control over the animals. But despite the power that God gave us through the use of the tongue as an instrument to achieve many of our purposes, it is almost impossible to control it, even in much simpler things like human communication.

In relation to this the **word of God** tells us:

"But no man can tame the tongue, which is an evil that cannot be bridled, full of deadly poison. With it, we bless God and Father, and with it, we curse men, who are made in the likeness of God. From the same mouth proceed blessing and cursing. My brethren, this must not be so."

With the tongue we can heal the deepest wounds, or plunge a dagger into the depths of a brother's spirit; with it, we can sing with joy to God and to men, or we can cast spells and curses; but what we must be clear about is that from a source of water cannot emanate fresh and saltwater at the same time; so it is with the tongue and everything that comes out of it.

The tongue is not tamed by its muscular representation alone. It is tamed through the brain, which in turn is directed by the mind (the captain), from which emanate the thoughts and intangible codifications by which the brain dictates direction to the tongue to execute the action of speaking.

Therefore, the mind is our starting point to be able to begin to gain victory over this very special member of the body, after knowing its use in-depth.

If our mind is connected with the source of Light that is never extinguished, if our thoughts are connected in their totality with the source of radiant light, if they have radiated towards the tongue the strength and brightness transmitted by its source, our neighbor will listen to the words that come out of your mouth as water that will quench his thirst.

As long as we have weak minds, as long as we do not have our being in order, as long as we do not purify our thoughts by seeing and hearing things pleasant to the soul; as long as we do not allow God to direct our being totally and we are subjected to vain talk, exposing a lack of courtesy and kindness; as long as we have less communication of body and spirit between us and less tolerance in verbal treatment, we will continue to burn great forests with this small fire.

Therefore, it is important to purify our thoughts, to be able to express them subtly by using our tongue.

Leadership and Testosterone

Sometimes we become weak in the flesh, while maturity and knowledge approach our lives. As we live and create experiences, our body and soul accumulate too many tasteless tastes; usually, they are situations, decisions, and actions that make noise through time.

If there is no early correction, there may be later fatalities that can be translated into the mistakes we may very possibly make by not preparing ourselves spiritually and physically at certain times of life. The challenge is to overcome temptations, even those that look like miracles and come out of nowhere.

The Bible narrates in great detail, and for special reasons, the story of King David and Bathsheba (The Bible).

David and Bathsheba, who, at the end of the story, ends up being the mother of the wisest and greatest king of all times, King Solomon.

In the details, we see that by that time, King David had several wives and almost twenty sons, and another number of daughters. He was head of the Jewish people, the greatest in history, and his army was in the midst of a war, of which he, as leader and God at the head, had already delivered his people from many.

Even so, David found time, energy, lividity, and mental relaxation to have a love affair. That is nothing more than the demonstration of his talent and qualities, despite the mistake.

Imagine the temptation of the King, when stressed and worried about all the responsibility that rested on his shoulders at that moment, he climbs to the roof of his house to dissipate a little, and from above he sees a splendid and beautiful woman in the courtyard of his house, located below, taking a special bath in the nude that the Jewish Law commanded at that time for purification in the week that ended menstruation.

This was, for better or worse, a tempting and unexpected proposal for the leader, as if it were a matter of destiny; for the situation of that beautiful woman, not only indicated that she was fresh and perfumed, but also fertile and with a more intense need for manly warmth that she could not satisfy at home at that precise moment and perhaps never since her husband was at war fighting for the king. How ironic...!

In the end, the king sends for her and after that (imagine that), she becomes pregnant. This causes David to make several mistakes, such as premeditatedly planning the death of his faithful warrior and husband of Bathsheba and then making her his new wife. But God punishes him for it, turning his own family against him; then David repents, cleanses his heart and God forgives him, but two of his sons die and one of his daughters is raped by a half-brother.

In synthesis, this part of the story leaves us a teaching; that in spite of having God in our favor we must respect His parameters and be sincere in His eyes, so it is necessary to keep in mind that He assures us that "even the hairs of your head are numbered". This being so, we must ask ourselves:

What is the goal of our actions?

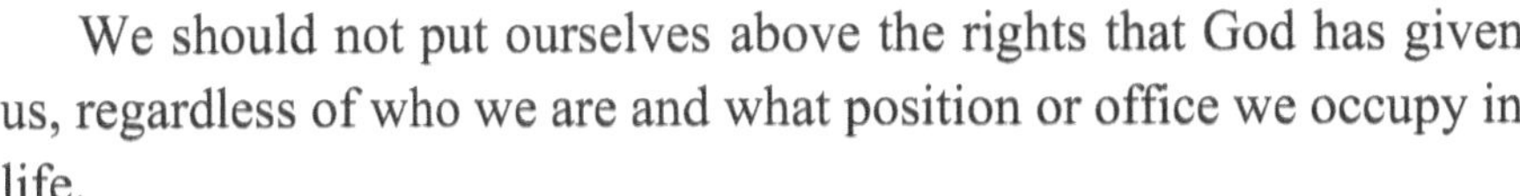

We should not put ourselves above the rights that God has given us, regardless of who we are and what position or office we occupy in life.

If it is true that David was king for many years in a reign of peace, it was merely due to his surrender to God and his faith in letting himself be used by Him; and above all, because of his sincere and devoted inner love towards God and towards men, which made David shine before the eyes of the world from a very young age, and mainly to prepare himself for God's purpose, which was to place him as the future head of his chosen people.

Some of the great errors that were committed were those that we have mentioned, but God by His love and grace for David made him correct his faults and humble himself before Him as many times as He considered necessary. God cleansed all that was part of the dross of David's mistakes, as an imperfect man.

It is necessary to be determined, to have a defined path, and to follow it without leaving the route.

We must make sincere sacrifices before ourselves and God, in order to feel and see the results of obedience.

We must resist temptation, just as Christ did in the desert. We must know how to take and leave, choose and reject, for the lines drawn by the leader of evil are thin and tailored to our thoughts, to bring confusion to our choices.

We must be cautious and know how to avoid what we know will come at some point, and if it comes without realizing it, simply let God in our rest remove that which does not come from Him. We can test God in His promises, because the simple fact of our interest, will put direction to our concerns.

And if we have a couple or family, we should never leave aside the blessings and responsibilities that God gives us. We are the models of our children, and they will set the end of our cause.

The word says: *"you shall leave your father and mother and be joined to his wife, and you shall be one in body and spirit".*

When we reach the ultimate journey to our goal, if we do not see the tree grown and taste of its fruit, we will never know how our sowing tastes; therefore, we must work to obtain excellence of character as husband and father, or as wife and mother, regardless of whether you are king or subordinate.

Perhaps you are left with more questions, such as the following:

Do miracles happen to those who do not need them?

Can a miracle that God has given you harm someone else?

All those who receive a blessing without it affecting anyone negatively, and where what is received allows one hundred percent of the goodwill of the environment to you, then we can be confident that such results come from God.

Despite his shortcomings as a man, David repented, asked for forgiveness, and was pure and clean of heart.

Let us remember that ***Jesus said***:

"Blessed are the pure in heart, for they shall see God.

shall see God.

Likewise, Christ said very clearly in a prayer the summary of all that we have reflected upon:

"By their fruits, you shall know them...Thus every good tree bears good fruit, but the bad tree bears bad fruit. Every tree that does not bear good fruit is cut down and thrown into the fire."

Encouragement in a Leader

> **Encouragement is the battery that infuses electricity into the whole body and spirit.**

"Have I not commanded you? Be strong and courageous. Do not be afraid; do not be discouraged, for the Lord your God will be with you wherever you go." **Joshua 1:9.**

Sometimes you wake up anxious, confused and you don't understand anything, everything gets cloudy just when you thought it was going perfectly.

I will share this experience with you:

Just a few days ago in a business meeting involving an investment of millions of dollars with those who were supposed to be my partners in a large community project, we had reached an agreement where they made the promise that they would invest in this project to execute and materialize what had been several years of planning, expenses, significant economic investments, studies, meetings, thoughts, group efforts and above all time, a lot of time...

This project was the largest, most ambitious, and most important of my entire career, up to that moment. My architect partner and I had

put everything we had into this project, which resulted in a groundbreaking industrial design patent.

Suddenly, one night, I received opposite news: from one moment to the next, the partners had changed their words, precisely in the process of drawing up the legal documents. I was stunned, frustrated and with my mind clouded.

The next day, at 08:00 a.m., without having been able to get to sleep. m, without having been able to sleep for almost the whole night, after my respective meditation, my reading, and the usual prayer, I took a book which I had read long ago, and as soon as I went over the underlined pages I remembered and understood again that I should not be cloudy if I was already so close to the objective, that I should not think, nor let negative thoughts dominate my mind with such a stupid and absurd idea, as to think that after so many years of swimming to a place of dry land, I could not swim a little further, even when God had shown me the shore.

Even so, things did not turn out as I had imagined, and the years that followed gave me a great lesson in life, a lesson that has served me greatly today and for which I can say that I am a new man.

I understood that the spirit is that power, that organic vigor that you feel and that you let feel to everyone that you animate through your same sphere. Encouragement is what drives us to action and to infuse others with that positive moral energy that sometimes explodes in some of us and which, as it matures, allows us to create an atmosphere full of results.

The synthesis of the writings of eminent sages that I reviewed that day left in my mind something like this:

The greatness of spirit is a fundamental requirement for leadership and good management; he who possesses it will be incited to greatness in all its dimensions.

Good courage enlarges the heart and elevates the thoughts, it grows within you with self-will full of generosity and kindness to others; even if it is limited and with adverse circumstances, it always excels where it is found.

A great example of the greatness of spirit in the history of the world from its beginnings is **Joseph** (in the Bible, see Genesis), who thanks to the great encouragement given by God through the Spirit, was always positive and with his mind alert and clear. Thus, he was pleased in Pharaoh's eyes, and was taken from prison to be the head of Egypt. Or as the book of the Dominican preacher Saulo Hidalgo says, Joseph was taken from the well to the palace, and unquestionably, a fundamental part of his character was his greatness of spirit.

In the same way and proving the solidity of a great spirit, more than 1,900 years of history later, we see Steve Jobs, a leader who applied greatness of spirit, who worked hard for many years taking it with him and giving it to others, until his death.

This marked his success and makes him still permanent today as one of the great entrepreneurial leaders full of courage in history because that is what he sowed in his descendants: the immense legacy left to the new generation of the 21st century.

Walk with courage, apply in your mind and spirit the rest, to which Jesus referred, in everything that you cannot solve at this very moment, and go out ready to give your best face, but that there is no hypocrisy in it, but that God does it through the Spirit, as he did with Joseph.

Appearance and Look

"But the Lord said to Samuel, "Do not consider his appearance or his height, for I have rejected him. The Lord does not look at the things people look at. People look at the outward appearance, but the Lord looks at the heart." Samuel 16:7.

In studying ancient wisdom, we see that most things are not seen for what they are, but for what they appear to be. The depth of what they are is only measured by intimacy, or daily use and practice, and the deeper the depth, the fewer people swim in it.

To be worth and to know how to show it is to be worth twice as much.

More on this: beware, let us not confuse knowledge with worth; for, to show knowledge is imprudent without understanding why, which inevitably can be seen with ostentation. But, knowing how to show courage organically will lead us to such positive results that we will elevate our spirit and naturally say something like what Daniel said in his book of the Bible, and we will surely always get the same positive result that he had.

Daniel ch.1 verse 8-20: This is what happened:

"But Daniel resolved not to defile himself with the royal food and wine, and he asked the chief official for permission not to defile himself

this way. Now God had caused the official to show favor and compassion to Daniel, but the official told Daniel, "I am afraid of my lord the king, who has assigned your food and drink. Why should he see you looking worse than the other young men your age? The king would then have my head because of you."

Daniel then said to the guard whom the chief official had appointed over Daniel, Hananiah, Mishael and Azariah, "Please test your servants for ten days: Give us nothing but vegetables to eat and water to drink. Then compare our appearance with that of the young men who eat the royal food and treat your servants in accordance with what you see." So he agreed to this and tested them for ten days. At the end of the ten days they looked healthier and better nourished than any of the young men who ate the royal food. So the guard took away their choice food and the wine they were to drink and gave them vegetables instead.

To these four young men God gave knowledge and understanding of all kinds of literature and learning. And Daniel could understand visions and dreams of all kinds. At the end of the time set by the king to bring them into his service, the chief official presented them to Nebuchadnezzar. The king talked with them, and he found none equal to Daniel, Hananiah, Mishael and Azariah; so they entered the king's service. In every matter of wisdom and understanding about which the king questioned them, he found them ten times better than all the magicians and enchanters in his whole kingdom."

God blessed, outwardly and inwardly, and greatly, the four young men who decided to follow His way and trust in His promises.

And if we continue reading the story of Daniel, we will see how God gave these young men intelligence and understanding to comprehend all kinds of books and science.

They were beautiful in God's sight and He then made them much more beautiful in the eyes of men. Obedience was the complement for each one to become great and complete men of faith in the world in which they lived, and it was the grace that God saw in them that made the radiance of their bodies shine more brightly than ever, even in the fire through which they passed.

Thus, many will follow that light which they could not understand, but which fascinated their minds; for, well says the word: *we Christians will be a spectacle before the world.*

In the same way, we can refer to what the Bible says about the appearance that Joseph, David, and Solomon had. God in his grace transforms even our countenance, allowing our faces to shine like a ray of light. He did the same with Moses in front of his people.

We must understand then that for this to happen, God must be amid our purposes and goals; for, while it is true that appearance and appearance are given by him, they are important instruments for the success of an entrepreneur and a fundamental issue for those whom God chooses to be so, as he did with Samson.

Let us never believe that our appearance and image will change in any way because of the price of what we wear, or because it is a product of some brand that stands out on our person.

Everything that does not belong to natural beauty is superfluous.

However, there are special moments that merit a difference, but they are still just moments. The true appearance is seen in the face, and the outward appearance is affirmed by the inward appearance; which is the light that our eyes denote.

Christ said well:

"We are the light of the world...and our eyes are the lamp of the body." Through the eyes we shall see the innermost aspect of a human being; and if God is in him, he who knows the Spirit shall see his light."

Let us be an example of outward appearance and appearance. This will be the best recommendation from within us to those around us. For, to attain greatness of spirit, spiritual, mental and bodily balance is essential.

Jesus said*: "the body is the temple of the spirit...",* and it should be treated as such, giving it an aspect of importance so that it shines in its natural appearance.

A Sophisticated Character

Nothing is cooked in the lukewarm. In the very cold, preserves lose their properties; but in the very hot, gold is refined.

In the Bible; ***Revelation. Ch.3:14-19***. God says:

"I know your deeds, that you are neither cold nor hot. I wish you were either one or the other! So, because you are lukewarm—neither hot nor cold—I am about to spit you out of my mouth. You say, 'I am rich; I have acquired wealth and do not need a thing.' But you do not realize that you are wretched, pitiful, poor, blind and naked. I counsel you to buy from me gold refined in the fire, so you can become rich..."

This is how God refines us, like gold. Thus, he expresses it in many verses, for it is his means of attaining our perfection in character and then enabling us to shine with a natural light, which is not quenched by the wind and shines much brighter with the rays of the Sun.

But to reach this beautiful conclusion we must thoughtfully understand certain important things:

Do you know how gold is refined?

To arrive at refining, we must allow ourselves to be found by the refiner. We must be willing to submit to his ways and the details of the development process that leads to becoming a valuable piece of gold for the world.

Somehow, we all feel the need to belong and be part of something, so it is very difficult, in practical terms, to detach a piece of charred stone from deep within the earth and then melt it down. When that happens in our life, we feel that we are losing part of the body and that fire will eventually incinerate us.

But there is a key point: we are not stones. Beyond the symbolic, we have a mind and a spirit that allows us to choose, to think, to act, and by these means, God acts through us as he does with no other living being, for we are special in his eyes, because we are his most precious children.

And it is precisely this that characterizes the essence of all human beings, the ability to choose. Sometimes wise decisions are made and sometimes they simply do not work out as we expect. But from each one we learn, and from these experiences our being is nurtured, and as a result, our character is forged.

That is to say, in the end, not because we live at the speed of light, or because we have advantages over others in some areas of life, we will be able to fly the space and time required to forge a character with excellence and enter the light.

If we look for references from thousands of years ago, in the time of devout kings like Solomon, we find that God blessed the reigns of the Jewish people because of the devotion of their leaders; and likewise, He punished them when disobedience came from the powers of the evil kings but NEVER abandoned them.

In the end God says clearly in verse 19:

"Those whom I love I rebuke and discipline. So be earnest and repent."

That being so, I ask:

How many of us are prepared to endure the physical, mental and spiritual discipline that comes with our chosen path?

How many of us will have the humility and capacity to listen and act when God rebukes us?

How many of us will be able to see beyond the bubble that envelops us?

Let us go out into the world today with an attitude of kindness and change, let us try to seek the deepest, most accurate, and sincere inner answers to these questions; always having as a goal to increase the excellence of our character, in order to mold it and walk on a path of adventure, sacrifice, love, dedication, and humility of a true leader, with the strength of a father of a family, with the vigor of a prepared young man, with the passion of a hardened entrepreneur, with the vision of a prophet and his calling, with the character of an accomplished man, the recognition of a retired leader and the docility of a rested elder.

Charisma and Leadership

> *"Each of you should use whatever gift you have received to serve others, as faithful stewards of God's grace in its various forms."* **Peter 4:10**

As long as we are in grace our charisma will prevail and if we do not have this virtue, the one that exists will stand out.

The definition in the Spanish language found on the web of the word charisma, says:

It is the ability of certain people to motivate and arouse the admiration of their followers, thanks to a supposed quality of "personal magnetism."

Baltasar Gracian wrote in his book **"The Art of Prudence"** that:

"...charisma is the life of qualities, the breath of the soul, the soul of works, the most important of eminences. The remaining perfections are an ornament of the natural capacity, but the charism is of the perfections: it is even praised in thought".

We have seen, throughout history and up to our days, the development of this great virtue in many leaders, from characters like Moses, Joseph, Abraham, David and his harp, Solomon his son, Charles V, Prince of Persia, Alexander the Great, and all the philosophers of history, including artists, political leaders like

Abraham Lincoln and evangelists like Martin Luther, Ellen G. White, and Billy Graham, and revolutionaries. White and Billy Graham and revolutionaries like Martin Luther King, to creators and innovators of today's world like Henry Ford, Rockefeller, and Steve Jobs, who in the end are all entrepreneurs, and all are sealed by the virtue of charisma.

In the end, charisma is a natural gift given by God, but that does not imply that it can be misused, since, on top of that, God has given us free will. For this reason, we must be careful and disciplined.

Let us look at the example given in the story about Samson.

Many have heard of him, but very few know his original story since they have distorted it with fables and legends of today; but his original story will always be in the most truthful place where no one can ever capture the truth, in the Bible.

In this story we see a man full of a kind of super charisma concentrated in the physical aspect, a charisma that was misused, although in the end God's will is fulfilled; but in this case, the hero dies.

(See Judges 13-17)

Of course, our effort also has merit, because we are parabolically speaking sowers, and this is superior to the rules, it goes beyond the brightness and the general facilities.

Without charisma, everything beautiful dies and any quality lacks its essence.

Gracian said: "Charisma surpasses courage, discretion, prudence, and majesty. It is a practical shortcut to business and a delicate way out of any predicament."

And when we mature and understand where that charisma comes from, that being able to get out in front of something in life... When we understand the essence of such great virtue, the source from which springs the light we call charisma, we will see that we are directly connected to the Father.

Many like Gideon and the 300 (Yes! It was from where the story of that famous Hollywood movie *300* was taken), are taken by surprise and directed by God for specific missions at a specific time, while God works our courage through trials and demonstrations of his power.

And others he protects and directs from birth, giving them the virtue of charisma to fulfill the mission requested by our heavenly Father.

However, there is a conditional point: you must possess a vision so that people can be truly convinced, as I once heard it said: "with a map to infinity".

Human beings support ideas that are generally aligned with our roadmap and that are open to giving more people the opportunity to be part of it.

Perhaps I am a dreamer, as I have heard many say, but I believe and see shortly, and around the world, entrepreneurial organizations led by charismatic leaders and directed by God in a real way, like Gideon and the 300, are clear with their ideals and practices.

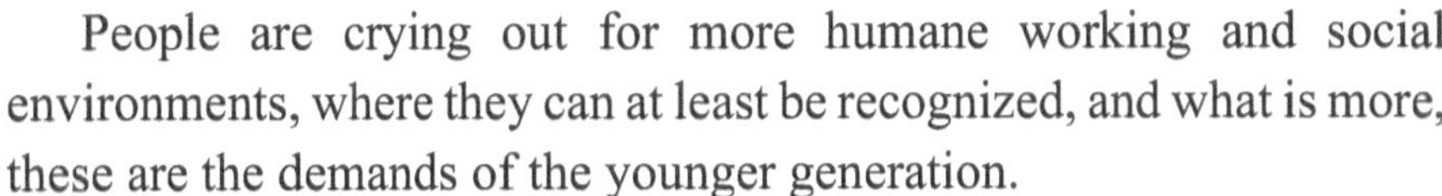

People are crying out for more humane working and social environments, where they can at least be recognized, and what is more, these are the demands of the younger generation.

Younger people are looking for more than an 8-5 pm job. They are looking for a job that has a purpose. And those who possess special talents must put them one hundred percent at God's disposal to achieve these ends. But to reach the goal we must initiate an inner change.

We must daily ask for God's guidance and blessing on our path to undertake; for the journey is long and uncertain for us. But clear and definite to Him. And as we turn to the Father, we will always see the trace of light emitted by the spotlight of His direction on the road we must travel to reach the expected destination.

In recent generations the talents at the service of God have been hidden, the charism is wasted and mercilessly prostituted. We have lost focus on what is true and have reached the point of wanting to see God as an image created by man and not the other way around. And this is a fatal error in the eyes of our Creator.

Let us seek and reflect on God's first two commandments.

Let us walk securely and confidently on the path of truth, for there we will stand firm no matter what comes; then let us undertake without fear, humbly bringing out our charisma and putting it in favor of others, to achieve our objectives with God's favor.

The Negative Effect of Ego

Although it may seem so, the ego does not belong to our being and to our essence as beings with a soul. It simply dwells in us just like the other attitudes and aptitudes that induce us to act erroneously, often unconsciously, and other times under individual internal struggles that some believers in their own judgment call spiritual struggle, while others call it trials.

We all have tribulations and problems as human beings, but it is not the passing situations that determine how we view or cope with difficulties, but the way in which these situations are faced and the positive thoughts we use to resolve them.

This, added to the patience and confidence with which a man or woman walks through life won by excellence, under a trusting obedience based on a simple but effective faith, is the formula to overcome problems.

Nothing that we build in the air will have a foundation to sustain itself, in the end, it will end up falling to the ground under its own weight; this is a law.

Our ego is so big and so influential in our decisions and inner thoughts, even in our actions, that it does not let us see beyond the personal bubble in which it envelops us.

If we look at people, we will notice those thousands of little things that we do naturally, which sink us more and more each day in this involuntary selfish condition. The "self" will always leave stains as we walk, which we call consequences, a matter that can have multiple results.

The best way to realize this and to be able to reflect is to contrast the way we used to live with the way we live now and would like to live.

When we let arrogance, self-complacency, vanity, or excessive self-confidence lead us to things like dressing up too much, constantly looking at ourselves in the mirror, working with excess in shaping our body, and not seeing the outside world, helping others and extending a hand to someone next to you who needs it; self-complacency, gluttony, anger, haughtiness, mockery, selfishness, the need to have and possess material things at whatever cost is necessary, will reign in us.

When I say necessary, I do not mean to be a participant in bad actions, because the worst action we can commit in the world is to harm ourselves by letting our being become the property of our ego.

In this regard ***King Solomon*** said:

"I have seen all the things that are done under the sun; all of them are meaningless, a chasing after the wind." **(See Book of Ecclesiastes).**

As a model of spiritual consciousness, Jesus always showed in his person, love, compassion, mercy, peace, humility, and intimate knowledge of spiritual truth. These characteristics are far removed from the human ego; even many great leaders in spiritual world history have tried to follow this lofty model to the letter.

It is our duty to strive to break those chains of self-centeredness that envelop us and govern our lives today. It is necessary that we leave aside the incessant consumerism that is killing us inside, because the more we have, the more we want, however, the emptier we are.

This is how we educate our children under this same wrong scheme, and the worst of all is that every day that passes the human being thinks more about his self, caring less about his neighbor.

A spiritual consciousness connected with that of the living God demands a great inner change, but once we begin the process it will be like a child learning to read and write.

It is a great and imperceptible gulf that exists between these two totally opposite states of being, and we must rely on our developmental process in order to achieve spiritual growth and move from one state to the other. This process will never be achieved by force, for it is purely organic.

Once we eliminate the ego from our being (which will take time) we will be men and women of spiritual substance. It is almost impossible for inner success to exist where there is no spiritual substance. Not all people are people who seem or appear to be, for many are totally wrapped up in the ego. In the end, their whims turn out to be wrong, for they lack a firm foundation.

Jesus also made reference to this when he spoke in parable, contrasting the house founded on a rock with the house founded on sand. Only truth and the search for excellence can give true prestige and a healthy interior where the substance is useful.

Men without sense do not reach old age and those who manage to arrive without it, die in misfortune.

When we finally decide to start this journey of inner cleansing, we will have to consciously renounce the previous life. It will be time to surrender and worship your creator, to have faith that you are not forgotten, to pray to God with fervor and true desire, to read the scriptures, for they will be a great manual.

In short: let us imitate the model of Jesus and wait with patience, he is our great example. He understood that the natural is essential for wisdom, and he showed us the true hidden reality of the soul when he said:

"...whosoever will come after me, let him leave all that he has, and take up his cross, and follow me."

Humility and reverence for the Lord will bring as its reward riches, honor, and life. *"In the paths of the wicked are snares and pitfalls, but those who would preserve their life stay far from them."* **Proverbs of Salomon**.

The Soul and the Self

The self fills itself, pours itself out, and remains empty. The soul is filled by the Spirit; because it is the true substance.

Since ancient times there has been a great battle within each of us as human beings. And as in every struggle, always one of the two (the Self or us) is the winner.

The Self is a great fighter, and we human beings have been in charge of giving it unconditional support so that it wins the battle. Some through ignorance, others through inconsistency, but many because of the evil contained in their thinking and acting, this being the most worrisome.

All things we have created for our self-indulgence, without being biased, include all the excesses of food, shopping, clothes, and luxuries; while hundreds of thousands die for lack of a piece of bread and water. How many people with extravagant earnings there are in this world, while millions remain unemployed or are unable to work, even though they have the desire and the training to do so. How many miserable payments for such difficult jobs, how much inequality in the world created by ourselves we have to see daily...

We must have clear within us a spirit of solidarity, kindness, gentleness, and love for others. And we must demonstrate to ourselves every step we take towards these virtues; because once you gain access to them, then, only then, the "self" will die and you will be able to see life from the perspective of the soul.

God promises us in His word that in Him we will be more than conquerors. However, for this to happen we must be in Him. But to reach Him we must pass through several steps. In the end, the channeler of all that comes from God is the Spirit. Once filled with Him, we will never again be empty.

It is necessary to know ourselves to be able to help ourselves and others. Wise men of centuries ago wrote something like this:

"A prudent man knows his character, intelligence, opinions and inclinations, one cannot be master of oneself if one does not first know oneself."

We know that there are mirrors for the face, but not for the spirit. This mirror must be a prudent reflection. When one is unconcerned with his outer image, he must preserve his inner image to correct and improve it.

He must know the strength of his prudence and perspicacity to undertake projects, check his tenacity to overcome risk, have measured his depth and his capacity for everything he has to overcome and undertake in life.

When we reach this point in our life consciousness, then we will be able to breathe differently and see from the same perspective other horizons. We will even contemplate colors that we did not see before and appreciate the beautiful and eternal in life from the perspective of the soul, and not of the "self". This is what is most significant.

I can tell you with certainty that even if your bodies feel full with the "self", it will be like being a box of synthetic foam, anyone who carries it will feel its lightness and, without having to open it, will know that it is empty.

We must adapt ourselves to go forward with an open heart while aspiring to eminence. Once attained, he will be twice eminent who hides his perfections within himself and not in the esteem of the "self".

The opposite path leads to applause.

Not long ago I read in an investigation a verse taken from a scroll said to be one of the lost gospels, and it went something like this:

"If those who lead you say to you, 'See, the kingdom is in heaven,' then the birds of the air will overtake you. But the kingdom is within you and without you. When you come to know yourselves, then you will be known and you will realize that you are children of the living Father. But if you do not know yourselves, you are plunged into poverty and you are poverty itself."

In the end, we all have to make the decision: either to continue under our strength and will or to seek the inner kingdom to reach the fullness of the soul. The encounter with our soul will eliminate all traces of ego, little by little, until we reach the excellence of character, which speaks for itself through our deeds and actions, making us pleasing to God's grace and to that of our neighbor.

God hopes that each one of us can see and be convinced that He is the only creator. He always meant that loving our neighbor represents a love that is pure and undefiled, a love that bears all things, that can bear all things, that endures all things, that understands all things, that knows all things, that forgives all things, that satisfies all things, that

gives all things, and that always, for the rest of our lives, is love without self-centeredness, a love that comes from the soul.

I end this chapter by quoting the **Apostle Paul** when he spoke to the Corinthians in his first letter, *9:24-27:*

"Therefore I do not run like someone running aimlessly; I do not fight like a boxer beating the air. No, I strike a blow to my body and make it my slave so that after I have preached to others, I myself will not be disqualified for the prize."

Go, by the way, be steadfast, resist, and let your soul be greater than your "self."

Excellence in everything

In a leader or entrepreneur, excellence is not a quality, but a talent; it is not an option, but a necessity.

To find excellence it is necessary to recognize, understand and live quality in every area of our lives. The greatest external and internal excellence in each one of us depends on quality.

It is the pursuit of excellence that drives us to strive for quality and perfection in everything we do, and although perfection is not achieved, it always drives us to be better. It is excellence in doing that brings us the satisfaction of doing our best.

Through excellence, many men who promised nothing, because they were ordinary, became extraordinary by putting that little extra at the service of others.

Through excellence, many men in history went from being simple waiters or slaves to being exalted by kings and princes full of complacency.

Likewise, through excellence, many people came to attract people to their projects after having served them.

By quality and excellence in living, working, and entrepreneurship, many men have been examples through the centuries to model many of today's businesses, families, goods, and services.

Excellence is not forced, quality is not exhibited. These are external consequences of the hard inner passion of a person who strives to do the best he or she can and to do the best for those around them.

To see on a more real plane a story of true excellence, here I briefly tell you the story of Cesar Ritz. None other than the creator of the famed Ritz hotel chain, which bears his name and is synonymous with excellence and quality:

"Ritz lived at the end of the 19th century when women began to demand equality in the workplace. At that time no woman of a good family dared to be seen dining in public, for example. However, Ritz persuaded some great women such as the Duchess of Devonshire and Lady Dudley to come to the dining rooms of his hotel.

Other women followed after this, and very soon, dining at the Savoy and the Carlton became a social duty.

Ritz introduced soft lighting to flatter women's faces so that they could show off their evening dresses; he planned his dining rooms so that women walking up a few steps would masterfully enter the room.

He conspired with his famous chef Auguste Escoffier to create a huge variety of dishes that would appeal especially to women. He also introduced in London, for the first time, soft music to be played during dinner. Ever the perfectionist, he chose Johann Strauss's orchestra to play for his guests.

A few months later he was fired. His employer commented that in the hotel business *"you have to have an aptitude and a style, and you have no trace of it."*

Ritz got another job as a waiter and was fired, again. He went to Paris where he got and lost two other jobs. His career began with the fifth job at a small, fancy restaurant near Madeline, where he rose from busboy to manager. He was only 19 when his employer invited him to be his partner.

For any young man, this would have been a great opportunity, but Ritz now knew what he wanted: the world of big names and lavish, epicurean parties.

He put away his aprons and walked down the street to the number one restaurant of the time, and agreed to work as a busboy, again from the back. He observed and learned everything, including how to serve food in a very pleasant way that pleased the eye and the palate.

In 1871 Ritz left Paris and for three years worked in restaurants famous for their attendance in Germany and Switzerland, by which time he was manager of a restaurant in the Alpine Hotel, known for its view and its cuisine.

One day the heater went out, almost at the same time as a message arrived that forty wealthy Americans were on their way to lunch. The temperature in the dining room was freezing...

Ritz wrapped in his overcoat ordered the tables to be placed in the room off the living room which had red curtains and appeared to be of higher quality, on four huge copper plateaus used until then to house palm trees he added alcohol and lit them, and fires were lit with bricks in the ovens.

When the guests arrived the room was tolerably warm and under each diner's feet was a brick in flannel. At the same time, the menu was a work of art for the cold, starting with a spicy consommé with pepper and ending with flambéed crepes.

This little miracle of ideas quickly spread like a rumor among the hoteliers' hangouts. Finally, it reached the ears of the owner of a large hotel in Lucerne who was losing money, and asked Ritz to be his general manager. Within two years, the 27-year-old peasant turned the hotel into a profit.

In 1892 he went to London to help the Savoy Hotel, which was experiencing financial problems. The public responded and the hotel was out of the red in a surprisingly short time. Going from room to room, Ritz was re-setting the hotel's beds to make sure they were well made with excellence, once when inspecting the dining room he smelled soap on glass and sent several hundred glasses to be re-washed.

The golden age of the Ritz ended with a quarrel between him and the managers. He returned to his beloved Paris and a dream he had treasured for years was fulfilled. He settled in the Place Vendome, the grandest of all Ritz hotels.

A few years later he opened the hotel that bears his name, the latter was the first building in England to use the steel beater construction that Ritz, in love with the Eiffel Tower, had insisted be included in the construction.

Eventually, he secured a group of financiers whom he joined to create the Ritz Handball Incorporation, which subsequently undertook the construction of most of the Ritz hotels around the world.

And this is a sample of a man who by his excellence achieved great things.

All those who want and strive for excellence need to clothe themselves in the perfectionism demanded by those souls who can and must only work with total passion and dedication.

The totality and perfection of anything in life is only two steps away from excellence, where the greatest talents of the genius that is at the service of others hide anxiously and impatiently to show themselves.

Over time I have read, seen, and heard so-called experts say and suggest that leaders should not attend to details. However, it is clear and notorious that the true leader is the one who is attentive to the important details, it is what distinguishes him and makes him, despite being a boss, a true leader with excellence.

All leaders of excellence that have existed in history, regardless of the area where they have excelled, have been detail-oriented, thoughtful, and attentive to quality and excellence in everything they do.

Excellence is dispersed in the appearance of stress and haste, in times of pressure. There can be no quality when distraction and work is being done. Much less will there be excellence when there is no meticulous attention.

Although a man may be considered, for example, the greatest orator or singer in the world, if the sound (the technical) is flawed and sloppy, no matter what he does, even if he forgets eloquence or a great voice, it will have no effect.

When you are going to do something always think of doing it to the best of your ability; otherwise, you will live walking on the path of mediocrity.

Leading a Healthy Life

To have a clean life is not an easy thing because it requires commitment, dedication, and total dedication to inner and outer reformation.

A clean life also requires a clean mind, not a holy mind, not a pure mind, but a clean mind. It must have been dirty before, of course, otherwise, it would not have the notorious relevance, for why clean what is not dirty?

When the mind begins to cleanse and rid itself of all worldly dirt, the spirit of a renewed mind and a vigorous attitude begins to arise within us, and at that moment we begin to be aware of the inner dust that we are removing and that we did not see before.

When the mind is clean and orderly then we begin to order and clean our understanding, which will then lead us to the entrance door where the cleansing of our spiritual room awaits us.

The moment we begin to cleanse the spirit of our stinkiest areas, our broken parts, our dusty desires, our frustrations, then the spiritual dirt begins to fall off one by one until our spirit is whitened, ordered, and ready to do its rightful part.

Once the mind and spirit have been cleansed through a time of maintenance, continual care, and discipline, it is time to focus on our external part.

Yes! It is not the other way around. First, we change, cleanse and tidy the inner man so that we can then change the outer appearance and everything around him. Mental cleanliness and spiritual clarity will give us the direction we must take to properly clean our body, which is the temple of the spirit and mind and where we dwell and will spend many years of our passing life.

The clean and tidy body of our concern and preoccupation of this kind denotes interest in doing. Thus, by attending to and keeping them clean in their entirety, we can also keep our environment clean.

Anyone who discovers the well-being that comes with a clean life will never want to lead a dirty life again, nor will his roof, his work, his relatives, or his life in general, because the recognition of the greatness hidden in this simple continuous action will give us the strength and conviction to never have a life like that again: a disordered present, a rotten mind or a putrefied spirit; but on the contrary, a clean, full life, full of good fruits, and in its total order, with an odorous and fragrant environment, a purified body, a whitened soul, a clean and renewed mind, which will be ready to exercise its true function in this world.

The only trace that such a life will leave will be the footprints and the path for future generations to walk on, always directed towards a better life.

Time to Act

The moment of acting is where a man's strength, preparation, ability, security, and dexterity are measured. It is at the moment of acting that we show what we are made of; but acting without planning and visualization of the action we will take will lead us to disappointment, even deeper than the one we were previously trying to get out of.

When we are sitting quietly and at rest, it is impossible to show our strength, much less feel the inner fervor that comes out of us, nor the deployment of action-oriented strength. But at this time we must visualize and plan calmly, do mental exercises and make mistakes in them again and again until we master them. This sometimes slow and perhaps tedious process is what guarantees success when it comes to action.

The moment to act must entail all the best of you, your resources, and creativity, sometimes the moment to act denotes a small initial action, but as we advance repetitively and cautiously, it will be the moment when our actions will become big, determined by the size and dimension that our responsibilities will have taken.

We will be inopportune and negligent if we are not ready when it is our turn to act, and we will be easily overcome by fear if we do not strengthen our spirit in prayer and persevering faith.

But the greatest strength lies in accepting, seeking, recognizing, and knowing how to operate when it is time to act under the power of God and the spiritual gifts; for, receiving such gifts will give us inner wisdom, even if we do not have much intelligence to recognize our strengths and fortify our character, as long as we work on our weaknesses, we can think calmly, while we prepare ourselves with wisdom to act diligently at the opportune moment.

Between the spirit and the body

The spirit is always ready to grow with greatness, while the body drives it to decrease by temptations.

The constant struggle between our spiritual being and our body is merely due to sin. When the body pushes us to the opposite side of the deepest desire, we allow ourselves to be dominated by superficial desire, and the distraction of what is not pure and healthy invades us.

This is due to the decrease of human values in the world, which is the consequence of the total ignorance of the personal growth of each one.

How can we grow in knowledge if we neither seek it, nor consume it, nor acquire it?

How can we overcome the force that pushes us to be worse, if we do not try to be better every day?

The whole root of the problem lies in what we have become as human beings; for if we are God's special creation, with a mind made in His image, then something is very wrong.

We can see all animals in harmony with their natural purpose, all of them seemingly living happily in automatic; however, we who being God's special creation are designed and connected to the infinite and divine source cannot be in harmony and order even with the people we love; so why is this?

What pattern is this that stifles the hope and future of so many millions of people?

Why have we let sin take control over us if Christ solved that problem long ago?

If the personal and spiritual development of each individual is not affected in a positive way, it is very likely that the world and its disintegration will affect your life forever.

Even after we have repented, even after we have been redeemed and asked for forgiveness, even after we have been forgiven, there remain those scars of what once was.

It takes years to change and grow as a person, to develop our inner self and grow in integrity, it takes years to find the right balance between body and spirit.

It all depends on the degree of depth and commitment you make.

Many of those who decide to take responsibility for this change will see the benefits of a progressive turnaround in their lives. They will endeavor to seek knowledge, education, faith, and the successful development of a new man or woman with discipline in pursuit of an unblemished purpose, which is the best sign of true inner development in a person.

Art and Wisdom

Art is whatever you let out, wisdom is whatever you let in and can apply.

Both are extraordinary in the soul of a man and both make the smallest seed great.

The art of wisdom is knowing how to make the best decisions for the journey of this life, those that will give you joy, those that discipline you to develop the necessary gallantry as a leader of your life; those that will lead you to prosperity, well-being, and good health, to enjoy a full life.

The Bible tells us, in the book of Kings, that when God told King Solomon to ask Him for whatever he needed to grant his request, Solomon was still very young, just assuming his position as King and maximum authority in Israel, full of dreams and desires, his only request to God was: *"My Lord, give me wisdom"*.

Wisdom gives us the ability to be excellent in our artistic branch, wisdom gives us the ability to acquire the right knowledge and to safely apply what we have learned.

Through art and wisdom, the greatest men in history have made themselves relevant to the world, and through it, the advances of science and the arts are growing at the speed of light.

By the art of thinking calmly, the wisest decisions are developed in the mind of a human being and by the ability to carry out our art our wisdom is defined.

Precision is given only by dedication, just as wisdom comes only from God, and to know it we must know Him. To know Him is not to know that He exists and, much less, to see Him from afar; to know Him is to speak to Him, to listen to Him, to know that He has us and that we want to express Him.

The Lord is wisdom and intelligence itself, so in essence, everything that is attached to these two greatness in the human being must be completely attached to the craftsman creator of them, because in Him, they are.

When art becomes inspired wisdom, its light will shine organically and imposingly upon the heart and soul of the one whom God blesses.

When a leader discovers the art of wisdom, he may perhaps make mistakes and many times fall into sin, but his center will always be God and his actions will be a work of art for all the spectators around him.

And when our being strives to become holy, healthy, and wise, the results of each step taken towards this goal will be a living sample of the art and wisdom of God in us.

Patience or Impatience in Entrepreneurship

When a man or woman assumes a position of entrepreneurship or leadership, that is, anything that involves responsibility for a family, a group, a company, a community, or a country, he or she must prepare for all that will come with keeping afloat and growing what has been entrusted to him or her.

There is nothing more important and fundamental in this whole process than patience because there is no magic formula or material resources that can accelerate a process that must be crossed over time. This must be taken into account for the healthy development of the leader or entrepreneur and his group.

In the laws of nature, the creator always dedicates a season of time for each thing, and each thing bears fruit in its own time. Seasons develop in the process of harvesting, and at the end, when everything is ready, the sweet fruits can be harvested.

Patience is not an attribute acquired by education, nor is it the hypocritical political diplomacy labeled as patience.

Patience is not given by time, nor meditation, nor yoga, nor Buddhism, nor any religion, patience does not come from the emotions nor from the soul, patience is given by God.

The Bible says about patience:

*"...But the fruit of the Spirit is love, joy, peace, forbearance, kindness, goodness, faithfulness..." See **Galatians 5:22**.*

The most relevant leaders and entrepreneurs, respected and studied by us, almost all have received patience from above, and they all know that it is not acquired, but it is a fruit that is born from the careful cultivation of the soul.

The leader who knows how to lead with patience, as well as the entrepreneur who knows how to wait for the natural process of each thing, in suffering, in mistreatment, is the one who endures and continues with a simple faith, the one who recognizes that perhaps many of his past mistakes were due to his impatience and that he has only been able to live patiently the processes in which the almighty God has been with him; those are the leaders and entrepreneurs who learn and can transcend in time successfully.

Let us look at men like King David, his son Solomon, Jesus the Christ, the greatest of all times; Martin Luther. Let us look at Gandhi, Nelson Mandela, and Martin Luther King, they are living proof in history that the patience made to withstand all trials only comes from God.

We may have vigorous personalities, sometimes be volatile in temperament as was the apostle Peter, sometimes we will act with madness and despair like many great misunderstood geniuses of history, and sometimes we will be imprisoned by moments of impatience, anxiety, or despair because in the end, we are human beings; but I firmly believe that God can give us patience to overcome eventualities in time.

Finally, let us remember that even if we experience difficult moments that make us impatient during the process of life, through leadership and a real, honest, respectful, and committed to those we serve and to God, we will be able to achieve stability.

It will not encourage us to acquire daily in prayer, as leaders and entrepreneurs, a dose of the patience that only God gives us, through sincere communication and total dedication to Him.

Conclusion

We are not perfect, but we can achieve many things if we know how to choose which path to walk and how we will walk.

We will always need a manual to be able to walk better on God's path; but remember that no manual will tell you what specific things will happen to you along the way, it simply prepares you for this encounter. If it is a good manual, it can best describe all the alternatives. My manual is the word of God.

Let us have the conviction, regardless of the circumstances, that there is a God in heaven who watches over our welfare. Let us seek, question, and learn so that we can see spiritual things with better discernment.

Although we may not want to acknowledge it, we are in our essence spiritual beings divinely endowed with virtues, such as charisma, character, judgment, prudence, love, mercy, strength, faith, courage, courage, confidence, etc.

These virtues help us to differentiate reality from the illusion in which we currently live, where our perception of things has been inverted; and we cannot turn a blind eye to something as factual as the fact that the death of the human body is part of us and that none of us have the answer to what will happen after we die.

But if we know how to choose our instruction manual and know clearly who our captain is and what our starting point is, we will surely live much better at every stage of our lives.

It is important to be aware of where we are heading in life, so that we will have a better chance of achieving a great end, no matter what it may be; we will also have the conviction and inner satisfaction that as human beings we have given our all and that no result, whatever it may be, can be less than that for which we have given all our effort.

The good tree bears good fruit, the bad tree cannot bear good fruit.

Be careful not to confuse the fruits with the fertilizer, nor with the decorative jar in which the tree is planted.

For example, money and vanity are NOT considered or understood as fruits, and much less can they be placed above the children and the family, which is our true and only inheritance, and in itself, they represent that which comes directly from the seed of the trees, which is the result of the nutrition obtained in time by the sap itself that transmits sweetness, to then feed many more who will continue to receive and give from what they have received.

Finally, keep in the deepest part of your heart that you were created for a purpose, so go for it with faith and without fear, and remember that you were created to triumph!

About the Author

Edgar Hernandez Rizek

A YOUNG ENTREPRENEUR FROM A SMALL CARIBBEAN ISLAND WHO HAS ACHIEVED PROFESSIONAL, PERSONAL, AND FAMILY SUCCESS AGAINST ALL ODDS.

My beginnings as an entrepreneur were very difficult, without money or a sense of direction of what I wanted to do with my life, without a defined talent, nor a father or mentor to guide me, so I started at 21 years old in the summer of 2001; But the search, the desire and the effort to find the meaning of my existence led me on the path that was predestined for me, in this journey I have had great ups and downs, I have lived in scarcity and abundance, in fame and the unknown and in happiness and sadness, which have given me maturity, strength and knowledge to undertake and successfully overcome the toughest tests. Today I have more than 15 years of being professionally free and working in things I love to do and most importantly a beautiful family which is today my greatest treasure.

In the last 5 years, I have turned my life around, I have helped other people to transform their lives, I have studied through self-taught techniques more than 315 books on leadership, business, family, personal and spiritual growth, as well as seminars and specialized courses with international experts, allowing me to be more useful to help many who like you dream of starting something new.

I ASK YOU A FAVOUR

I would like to ask you a small but big favor for this book to reach more people, and that is that you value it with your sincere opinion on the platform where you bought it.

I know from experience that this is the best way for the message to reach hundreds of thousands of people, and your grain of sand will be of great value to achieve it.

Also, as a reader, you will be helping me with the organic marketing of this book, because at this moment I am excited to start writing the next book for you.

God bless you.

Edgar.

WOULD YOU LIKE TO BE PART OF MY NON-PROFIT ORGANIZATION?

EDGAR HERNANDEZ RIZEK is the founder of Aprendedor Digital, a 100% online training academy that aims to help low-income Latin American youth with a desire to grow, to form an entrepreneurial mindset, find their life purpose, develop their leadership and create their businesses through their values."

PURPOSE AND OBJECTIVE

"To help train low-income Latin American youth to achieve an entrepreneurial mindset, providing them with tools and new knowledge to develop their leadership as professionals and entrepreneurs."

If you would like to be part of our team of collaborators, or you would like to sponsor some of our students with donations, or even if you are someone who needs to join our academy as a student, please write to me at:

E-mail: edgar@edgarmentor.com

E-mail: info@aprendedordigital.org

Bibliography

- Bible: New International Version (NIV)

- The art of war.

- The Art of Prudence: Baltasar Gracian

- Ellen G. White: Devotionals

- Greatness for each day: Stephen Covey.

- Ortega y Gasset's Phrases.

- As a man thinks: James Allen.

- Sentences of Ralph W. Emerson.

- Phrases of Mahatma Gandhi.

- Deepak Chopra: The Third Jesus.

- Writings of Shakespeare